Bede the Venerable

Twayne's English Authors Series

George Economou, Editor
University of Oklahoma

TEAS 443

Bede's *Historia ecclesiastica*
Cambridge University Library MS Kk. 5. 16 ("The Moore Bede"),
fol. 44v., the beginning of Book III, chap. 1.
By permission of the Syndics of Cambridge University Library.[1]

Bede the Venerable

By George Hardin Brown

Stanford University

Twayne Publishers
A Division of G.K. Hall & Co. • Boston

Bede the Venerable

George Hardin Brown

Copyright © 1987 by G.K. Hall & Co.
All Rights Reserved
Published by Twayne Publishers
A Division of G.K. Hall & Co.
70 Lincoln Street
Boston, Massachusetts 02111

Copyediting supervised by Lewis DeSimone
Book production by Janet Zietowski
Book design by Barbara Anderson

Typeset in 11 pt. Garamond
by Modern Graphics, Inc., Weymouth, Massachusetts

Printed on permanent/durable acid-free paper
and bound in the United States of America

Library of Congress Cataloging in Publication Data

Brown, George Hardin, 1931–
  Bede, the Venerable.

  (Twayne's English authors series ; TEAS 443)
  Bibliography: p. 136
  Includes index.
  1. Bede, the Venerable, Saint, 673–735. 2. Authors, Latin (Medieval and
modern)—Biography. 3. Authors, Anglo-Saxon—Biography. 4. Christian
saints—England—Biography. 5. Anglo-Saxons—Intellectual life. 6.
Civilization, Anglo-Saxon. I. Title. II. Series.
  PA8260.B76 1987   878'.0209 [B]   86–25834
  ISBN 0–8057–6940–4

Contents

For Phyllis and Heidi,
who assisted with their love and labor

About the Author

Born in Denver, Colorado, in 1931, George H. Brown did his undergraduate studies as a Jesuit at St. Louis University, where, after gaining an advanced degree in philosophy, he received an M.A. in English, studying Renaissance literature under Walter J. Ong, S.J. In Innsbruck, Austria, he studied theology for four years under Jesuit professors Karl and Hugo Rahner and Josef Jungmann. After further studies in Europe he went to Harvard for his Ph.D. in English, writing his thesis on Christ the Warrior-King in Old English literature, directed by Morton W. Bloomfield. He learned paleography from Chauncey Finch at St. Louis University (classics) and Malcolm B. Parkes of Keble College, Oxford (medieval English). Following two years' teaching at St. Louis University, Brown took up a post in the department of English at Stanford University, where he has continued since 1971. He teaches Old and Middle English language and literature, history of the English language, postclassical Latin, monasticism, humanities, and paleography. He is a member or officer in local, national, and international professional organizations, and is a collaborating editor of the Bulletin Codicologique of *Scriptorium.* His research has been mainly in Old English literature and theology, Anglo-Saxon history, and paleography, re sulting in articles and essays on *Beowulf,* Cynewulf's *Christ II,* Old English verse, the tenth-century English Benedictine reform, Chrétien de Troyes's *Yvain,* and several on medieval manuscripts. In his neighborhood he is known simply as Austin and Malcolm's dad.

Preface

When Bede, called "the Venerable" since at least the ninth century, completed *The Ecclesiastical History of the English People* in 731
and appended to it a bibliography of his voluminous writings, he
knew that he was leaving a large legacy to his community and his
nation; but he could not have known how much that legacy would
be treasured, used, copied, imitated, and plundered by admiring
generations. He immediately became one of the first and greatest
of English writers. In our own era scholars have awarded him the
titles of father of English scholarship, of English history, of English
literature, indeed, of the Middle Ages.[1] An initial sampling of his
writings may not convince the novice that Bede really deserves these
accolades. His works are largely either technical, theological, or
ecclesiastical; they are encyclopedic and written in medieval Latin.
Even granting that his Latin productions are prodigious, many of
these are at least partially derivative and contain ideas and statements
borrowed from Fathers of the Church and earlier authorities. Despite
his contemporary reputation as a vernacular poet and translator, we
possess no English composition indubitably his. What justification
is there for including the Venerable Bede in Twayne's English Authors Series, if he composed most of his works in Latin and the
most we have in Old English is a five-line poem that may be his?
The answer is, he was a great English writer. First, as the title
History of the English People and various remarks in his other works
demonstrate, he was English and thought of himself as English,
and not just a member of the clan or kingdom of Northumbria.[2]
Second, as to great, his nearly forty works (many of them in more
than one book), on nearly every major subject then known, make
him one of the most learned and prolific authors that England has
produced. His works on literature and poetics, exegesis, and history
set new standards for his age and for ages to come. As to the fact
that we have none of his English works, if we possessed only Marvell's
or Milton's numerous Latin writings and none of their vernacular
compositions, we should still call them English authors; so, for
Bede. Furthermore, Bede was a major conveyor of Roman Christian
literature to the unlettered Anglo-Saxon people, transforming and

melding the two cultures, Italic and Germanic, forever. That legacy we share today. These are some of the reasons why Bede enjoys the towering reputation he does. He did not have the original, theological mind of Augustine of Hippo; he did not have the ecclesiastical and political power of Gregory the Great; however, he did have extraordinary talents for synthesizing and presenting knowledge and for writing literature and history. No English author has been so universally admired for a longer time. This book should help explain why.

One might also ask, how can this monk, writing in an age characterized by a profound belief in God's activity in nature and human affairs, and convinced of his Christian mission to document that divine direction, appeal to the student of today? Ideally, the reader should meet Bede on his own ground and in his own milieu, but for a nonmedievalist that is a large order. Still, an examination of Bede's writing, despite its antiquity and antiquated assumptions (especially about the miraculous), soon reveals his enduring, splendid qualities: his candor, clarity, style, control, erudition, and reasonableness. Whether he is creating his own text in prose or verse, or assembling various sources and quotations in a unified commentary, or discoursing on poetry and metrics, on chronology and calculation, on scripture or history, Bede works with a sure artistic hand. Guided by a profound and humble commitment to truth tempered by a wise discretion, he makes it all his own.

Bede's corpus of extant writings, both prose and poetry, is the best witness of his worth. In addition, scholars have contributed much valuable information in recent years to aid our appreciation of his accomplishments. Nevertheless, since Charles Plummer's erudite introduction to his edition of the *History* in 1896, there has not been a scholarly book-length survey in English of all aspects of Bede's life and writings.[3] This study, drawing upon the enormously extensive and fruitful Bedan scholarship of the last hundred years, attempts to survey and evaluate Bede's career as educator, exegete, poet, hagiographer, biographer, chronologist, and historian. If the tone of this study tends to admiration, I can only respond that the subject has won it fairly. In that I join nearly everyone who has ever written about him. I hope this book will help persuade the student to read, understand, and enjoy Bede, who himself "always found it sweet to learn or to teach or to write" (*HE* V.24, p. 567).

Since the bibliography at the end is necessarily highly selective, the student pursuing further research on any topic should also refer to the bibliographic notes of individual chapters. In order that the book not take on the format of an annotated bibliography but maintain its focus on the subject, I have incorporated research findings of others within the body of the text sometimes by paraphrase, reserving for the endnotes credit and as full a citation as prudence and the editorial policy of this series allow. I have included in the notes and in the selected bibliography only items that are in my opinion genuinely significant for the particular topic. Parts of the book, especially those outside my specialization, are derivative; parts are original; all is my synthesis.

The following few abbreviations are used in the book for works referred to in the text: CCSL for Corpus christianorum series latina; CSEL for Corpus scriptorum ecclesiasticorum latinorum; *EHD* for *English Historical Documents, c. 500–1042,* vol. 1, edited by Dorothy Whitelock; *HA* for Bede's *Historia abbatum (History of the Abbots of Wearmouth-Jarrow),* edited by Charles Plummer in *Venerabilis Bædae opera historica* I. 364–87, translated by James Campbell, in *The Ecclesiastical History of the English People and Other Selections,* pp. 371–92 (page references are to Campbell); *HE* for Bede's *Historia ecclesiastica (Ecclesiastical History of the English People),* edited by Bertram Colgrave and R. A. B. Mynors; Keil, for Heinrich Keil, *Grammatici latini;* MGH for the series Monumenta Germaniae Historica; PL for Patrologiae cursus completus series latina, edited by J.-P. Migne; Plummer, for Charles Plummer, ed., *Venerabilis Baedae opera historica.*

The reader wishing to identify or find out more about Anglo-Saxons discussed should be aware that the spelling of nearly all Anglo-Saxon names varies considerably according to Old English, Latin, or modern English custom; thus are found Baeda (Old English), Beda (Latin), Bede (modern); Ædwin, Aeduini, Edwin; Eoforwic, Eboracum, York; in Gyruum, on Gyrwum, Jarrow. Furthermore, modern spellings of proper names also differ, e.g., Ecgberht, Ecgberect, Egbert; Oswiu, Oswy. Terms used for grammar, poetry, and exegesis follow the late classical and medieval, not modern, usage; thus, for example, "elegiacs" mean "distichs having the first line in dactylic hexameter and the second a pentameter," not "verses on a mournful subject."

In the preparation of this book my debt to scholars is obvious from the citations, and I wish I could thank all of them, from Bede through Plummer to the many great medievalists of our day. I am grateful for the excellent resources of the Green Library of Stanford and its staff, especially William Allan, James Knox, John Rawlings, and Elizabeth Green; and I wish to thank the dean of humanities and sciences, Norman Wessells, and his associates and assistants for furnishing members of the faculty with computers and support for our research and writing. My thanks too to the chairs and colleagues in the Stanford departments of classics, history, and English, who have helped in various kind ways, to Stephen Ferruolo, who read and appraised the whole manuscript, to Richard Hooker, who checked it for errors, and to Robert Rugg, who collated it. I appreciate the generous assistance I received at the British Library, the library of the University of London, the London Historical Institute, the Warburg Institute, the University Library and college libraries at Cambridge, and the Bodleian and college libraries at Oxford. I am obliged to the historians and paleographers Julian Brown of the University of London and Malcolm Parkes of Keble College, Oxford. I owe thanks to Stanley Greenfield for sending me an advance copy of parts of his and Daniel Calder's *New Critical History of Old English Literature* and for his reading this book in manuscript with care and critical eye even while he lay in the hospital, to Peter Brown who has inspired and enlightened me, to Glenn Olsen for his assistance through articles and correspondence, to Gerald Bonner for preventing me from perpetuating an error about Bede's education, to Martin Irvine for a reassessment of grammar in Bede's intellectual formation, to Paul Meyvaert for a number of suggestions, and, most important, to Roger Ray, who generously shared his impressive knowledge, publications, and prepublication materials with me. Finally, I owe my greatest thanks to my dear wife, Phyllis, who not only gave me a beautiful copy of John and George Smith's 1722 edition of Bede's *Ecclesiastical History* to encourage me in this enterprise but also has served as editor, corrector, loving provider of time and support, and as a stimulating critic at every stage of research and writing.

George Hardin Brown

Stanford University

Chronology

449   Traditional date of the arrival of Angles and Saxons in Britain (*HE* I.15), though archaeological finds suggest a somewhat earlier date.

597   Arrival of Saint Augustine of Canterbury, sent by Pope Gregory the Great to convert the English. Baptism of King Æthelberht of Kent.

627   Conversion and baptism of King Edwin of Northumbria.

640   Approximate date of Aldhelm's birth in Wessex.

663–664   The Synod of Whitby, at which the controversy over the date of Easter is settled against the Celtic faction in favor of the Roman group led by Wilfrid; subsequently he is made bishop.

669   Arrival of Theodore of Tarsus as archbishop of Canterbury and of his colleague, Hadrian of Africa, as abbot of the monastery of Saints Peter and Paul (later Saint Augustine's) nearby; they established a famous school (*HE* IV.2).

673   The Venerable Bede born during this (or perhaps the preceding or following) year in the Wearmouth area.

674   Benedict Biscop establishes the monastery of Saint Peter's at Wearmouth (afterward called Monkwearmouth; situated about fourteen miles northeast of Durham).

680   Relatives of Bede enter him at the age of seven as an oblate (monastic ward) under the care of Benedict Biscop.

682   Benedict Biscop establishes the twin monastery of Saint Paul's at nearby Jarrow under the abbot Ceolfrith, who probably brings Bede with him at this time.

692   Bede ordained deacon at the precanonical age of nineteen.

702   Bede ordained priest.

709   Death of Aldhelm, abbot of Malmesbury, then bishop of Sherborne.

731   Completion of Bede's *The Ecclesiastical History of the English People.* Several other major works done about this time.

734   Bede's Letter to Ecgbert, Archbishop of York.

735   Traditional date of Bede's death. Approximate date of Alcuin's birth in Northumbria.

794   Sack of Lindisfarne by Vikings.

804   Death of Alcuin, abbot of Saint Martin's, Tours.

867–870   Wearmouth-Jarrow destroyed by the Danes; restored c. 1074 by Aldwin, becoming cells to the priory of Durham.

Map of Bede's England from David Hill,
An Atlas of Anglo-Saxon England (Toronto: University of Toronto Press, 1981), p. 30.
Reproduced by permission of the University of Toronto Press.

Chapter One
Bede's Life and Times

Bede's career, 673–735, marks the supreme achievement of the advanced culture that developed from the mid-seventh to mid-eighth century in Northumbria. In the outer reaches of the known world, in the barbarian north far from Mediterranean civilization, late antique Christian culture found new life, when grafted onto the vital Germanic stock. This period of astounding learning and artistic creativity emerged from the preceding darkness of petty wars and bloody feuds. Bede's remotely situated Northumbrian monastery of Wearmouth-Jarrow emulated the older center of learning in the south, Canterbury; Bede's own reputation soon rivaled that of Canterbury's ostentatiously learned pupil and Bede's older contemporary, Aldhelm of Malmesbury, "the first English man of letters."[1] Soon after the quiet but brilliant career of its greatest writer, the glory of Northumbria disappeared, leaving us most of Bede's writings and a few letters from his students and admirers, some beautiful manuscripts (such as the Bible Codex Amiatinus) and manuscript fragments, and archaeological remnants and shards. But that did not happen before the passing of the torch to the school of York and its illustrious pupil Alcuin, who played a major role in kindling the Carolingian renaissance on the Continent.[2] If another culture succeeded in Mercia under the great but enigmatic rule of King Offa, it left very little trace. At the end of the ninth century King Alfred testified that when he came to the throne (871) learning was almost totally obliterated in England, following renewed political turmoil, religious and cultural apathy, and the Viking invasions.[3] After Alfred's valiant efforts and temporary success in stemming the tides of ignorance, learning once more receded until the great renaissance of the tenth-century monastic reform.[4] From start to finish (seventh to the eleventh century), learning, like life in Anglo-Saxon England, was a precarious affair. Historians have marveled that the Northumbrian cultural development could have occurred at all.[5]

The England of Bede

This achievement was made possible by two important factors, one political, the other religious. On the political scene, there was a modicum of social stability and a sufficient break in the interminable warfare to allow some culture to flourish. Some improvement of life, some prosperity, some progress followed the three centuries of desolation after the Roman withdrawal from Britain (410). Unceasing battles between Anglo-Saxons and Celts and among the Anglo-Saxon clans themselves gave way to interludes of peace.[6] In the religious sphere, Christianity brought a message of peace, education, and art in the service of God and humanity. The data we have about these developments comes largely from information furnished by Bede. Indeed, what we know today about his nation, its people and politics, its material conditions and social life, its struggles and wars, as well as its church and culture, derives almost entirely from Bede. What we know of his life and monastic career is also almost entirely known from his own modest testimony. Bede's principal historical work was intended, as its title informs us, to be an ecclesiastical history of the English, and to some extent like most early medieval writings it can from our own limited stance be accused of looking at reality "through stained glass windows."[7] Nevertheless, in its architectonic scope, intelligent plan, careful use of documents and reports by witnesses, it tells us most of what we know about early Anglo-Saxon history, sacred and secular, particularly of the seventh and eighth centuries. Some supplemental information is provided by a few concrete facts in saints' lives, such as those of Cuthbert, Wilfrid, and Guthlac, and by charters, codes of law, and annals.

These sources reveal ferocious power struggles among territorial kings. Although this Anglo-Saxon England has been traditionally described as a heptarchy (a confederacy of seven kingdoms), the reality was more complex, since there were in fact often more or fewer than seven kingdoms, some dominant and some subject, involving numerous chiefs, overlords, kings, and those kings called *bretwaldas* by the *Chronicle,* whose authority transcended their own territories and presaged a united nation.[8] Bede lists seven of these *bretwaldas* from the fifth to the seventh century; the last three (Edwin, Oswald, and Oswiu) are Northumbrians who held sway over the Mercians and the southern English during the one brief historical epoch of northern hegemony. The crown rested uneasily and briefly on any head bold enough to wear it. A few kings abdicated in favor of pilgrimage or monastic peace; but most of them died young and violently, as did their thegns (their noble companions, landholding retainers).[9] King Ecgfrith (ruled 670–85), whose largess established Bede's monastery, extended his kingdom into the territories of the Picts to the north and the Britons to the west and sent an army into Ireland to devastate part of Meath; but then, after his ambitions for control over Mercia were dashed by defeat near the Trent river (678), he and his army met a bitter end a few years later (685), trapped in an ambush at Nechtanesmere, near present-day Forfar in Scotland. His half-brother and successor, the well-educated Aldfrith, managed during his reign (685–704) to defend the kingdom and support the Church and education. Although Aldfrith was not as generous a contributor to Bede's monastery as Ecgfrith had been, he was honored by Aldhelm, who dedicated his letter-treatise on metrics to him, and by Bede who lauds him in the *Ecclesiastical History*. The political confusion after Aldfrith's reign did not hinder the continuation of a peaceable era in a land more typically characterized by war and terrorism. The wild Picts of what is now Scotland had agreed to a treaty and the traditionally hostile Celts of what is now Wales and Ireland were subdued. Until the rise of the Wessex kingdom after the battle of Ellendun in 825, the control of Anglo-Saxon England was divided between the weakening Northumbria and the more potent Mercia with its subject southern kingdom.[10] Despite therefore Northumbria's gradual weakening, there remained enough peace and prosperity in the realm for Bede's monastery to thrive for some years.

Monasticism and the English Church

When the Anglo-Saxons overran the country from the fifth century onwards, the British Christian church apparently made no attempts to convert the conquering peoples. Bede reports of the Britons, "To other unspeakable crimes, which Gildas their own historian describes in doleful words, was added this crime, that they never preached the faith to the Saxons or Angles who inhabited Britain with them" (*HE* I.22, p. 69).[11] In the late sixth century, however, Gregory the Great determined that the English should receive the word of Christ. After reviewing the life of this pope, who was so honored in England and so personally revered by him, Bede reminds his readers that Gregory "snatched our race from the teeth of the ancient foe and made them partakers of everlasting freedom by sending us preachers" (HE II.1, p. 131). Bede then relates the famous account of papal paronomasia:

We must not fail to relate the story about St. Gregory which has come down to us as a tradition of our forefathers. It explains the reason why he showed such earnest solicitude for the salvation of our race. It is said that one day, soon after some merchants had arrived in Rome, a quantity of merchandise was exposed for sale in the market place. Crowds came to buy and Gregory too amongst them. As well as other merchandise he saw some boys up for sale, with fair complexions, handsome faces, and lovely hair. On seeing them he asked, so it is said, from what region or land they had been brought. He was told that they came from the island of Britain, whose inhabitants were like that in appearance. He asked again whether these islanders were Christians or still entangled in the errors of heathenism. He was told that they were heathen. Then with a deep-drawn sigh he said, "Alas that the author of darkness should have men so bright of face in his grip, and that minds devoid of inward grace should bear so graceful an outward form." Again he asked for the name of the race. He was told that they were called Angli. "Good," he said, "they have the face of angels, and such men should be fellow-heirs of the angels in heaven." "What is the name," he asked, "of the kingdom from which they have been brought?" He was told that the men of the kingdom were called Deiri. "Deiri," he replied, "De ira! good! snatched from the wrath of Christ and called to his mercy. And what is the name of the king of the land?" He was told that it was Ælle; and playing on the name, he said, "Alleluia! the praise of God the Creator must be sung in those parts." (HE II.1, pp. 132–35)[12]

Gregory sent Augustine, who had been prior of his monastery of Saint Andrew in Rome, along with "several other God-fearing monks" (HE I.23, p. 69) to preach the gospel to King Æthelberht of Kent and his people. They arrived on the isle of Thanet in 597, and by Christmas had purportedly made over ten thousand converts.[13] A short distance from the new cathedral church in Canterbury, the missionaries built a monastery under the Roman patronage of Saints Peter and Paul, which afterwards became the burial place of Augustine, succeeding archbishops, and the kings of Kent. This little monastic group brought the Bible, literacy, and Mediterranean education to the southern English. Their imported literate culture was eventually to enfold the indigenous Anglo-Saxon culture with its pagan, heroically moving, oral literature.

The monk Paulinus, who arrived in the second group of missionaries with Mellitus from Rome in 601, was consecrated a bishop at Canterbury and became the apostle to the Northumbrian King Edwin, having served as chaplain to Edwin's Christian wife, Æthelberg.

The Irish monks from the monastery of Iona on the western coast of Scotland (founded by Columba in 563) had also been active preaching the gospel in the north. Later, monks from that foundation were to instruct King Oswald, Edwin's sainted successor in the faith. It was through the preaching activity of the Irish monks that Northumbria returned to the fold of the Church after the apostacy that had resulted from Edwin's devastating defeat by the Welsh king Cædwalla and his Mercian allies (632). Oswald persuaded them to establish a monastery at Lindisfarne under Aidan in 634.

Conversion in England took place generally without bloodshed and with relative speed. In contrast, both before and after the English conversion, many of the Continental peoples accepted the Christian faith only after stubborn resistance and violent persecution of the missionaries. Why was Christianity so readily, if at times only superficially and temporarily, accepted by the English? Certainly the inherent inadequacies of Germanic paganism, its incomplete pantheon and woefully weak and drearily fatalistic religion, had something to do with the easy and rapid spread of the gospel, "good news." Still, the eighth-century resistance of the Continental Germans, the Saxons and Frisians, to change in belief indicates that it was not just a religious vacuum that made English conversion easy. The memorable accounts in the *Ecclesiastical History* of the conversions of King Æthelberht and his Kentish people by Augustine (I.25–26, pp. 72–79) and of King Edwin, his court, and the high priest Coifi (II.12–14, pp. 174–89) demonstrate some of the factors at work in the conversion process. The missionaries' task was considerably expedited in both these instances by the influence of Christian wives in high places: in Kent, Æthelberht's queen, Bertha (daughter of the Merovingian king of Paris, Charibert), and, in Northumbria, her daughter and Edwin's queen, Æthelberg, made their husbands and courts sympathetic to the missionaries' message. Thorough prosletyzing of all the natives (not just the nobles) never did occur. Bede reports considerable backsliding in times of unrest, war, and famine. Still, towards the end of his life, Bede could optimistically declare in his *History* that "many of the Northumbrian race, both noble and simple, have laid aside their weapons and taken the tonsure, preferring that they and their children should take monastic vows rather than train themselves in the art of war" (*HE* V. 24, pp. 560–61). Even though we must qualify this picture in the light of his Letter to Ecgbert, an infraclerical document more candidly critical of contemporary religious life than the *History,* the fact is that Christian faith and mores were widely professed by the Northumbrians in the first half of the eighth century.

The two ecclesiastical traditions, the Roman brought by Augustine and his followers and the Irish, which continued among the Irish monks in England even after a large group of the Irish had gone over to the Roman way in Ireland, at first clashed over the disciplinary issues of calculating the proper date for Easter each year and of the form of tonsure to be worn by clerics. These religious disputes may now seem frivolous, but the fact that they could arouse such passionate responses among their adherents demonstrates that Christian asceticism is firmly embedded in history and local custom: the cut of the hair was an emblem that linked a monk to a venerable tradition, and the date of the most important feast in the Christian calendar, Easter, tied the liturgy with historical event. It was also, as Bede noted, a real annoyance that with the dating discrepancy between the Irish and Roman tradition, King Oswiu, who had been catechized by the Irish Lindisfarne monks, "had finished the fast and was keeping Easter Sunday, while the queen and her people were still in Lent and observing Palm Sunday" (*HE* III.25, pp. 296–97).[14] These matters were resolved for the English church at the Council of Whitby (663–64), where, under the suasive arguments of Wilfrid and with the support of King Oswiu against the Irish tradition upheld by the Lindisfarne bishop Colman, the Roman method of dating was declared correct. The paralyzing quarrel between Christians was settled (although some of the Celts would resist the Roman dating for another century), and the Northumbrian church could be united under the direction of Archbishop Theodore of Canterbury.

At the suggestion of the Neapolitan abbot Hadrian, Pope Vitalian had selected for archbishop of Canterbury the sixty-six-year-old Theodore, a native of Tarsus and an eastern monk of renown living in Rome, after the Anglo-Saxon nominee for the post died of the plague in Rome. Hadrian was sent to accompany Theodore to England (668). These two learned men, fluent in Greek as well as Latin, set new standards of learning at the monastery in Canterbury. After a visitation of the province, Theodore reorganized the episcopate, deposing some bishops and creating others. He summoned a council of the English church to establish ecclesiastical discipline (672), and organized the English church in such a way that, even with the reforms of the tenth century, it remained much the same structurally until the Reformation. *Theodore's Penitential* is the traditional name of a collection, made by his disciples, of canons and penances for religious offenses. His companion Hadrian became abbot of the monastery of Saints Peter and Paul; his successor Albinus furnished Bede with much of his information about Kentish history. Together, Theodore and Hadrian, so foreign to the English scene, proved most effective leaders, and their monastic school attracted for years the best talent in the south. Bede says of Theodore and Hadrian: "Because both of them were extremely learned in sacred and secular literature, they attracted a crowd of students into whose minds they daily poured the streams of wholesome learning. They gave their hearers instruction not only in the books of holy Scripture but also in the art of metre, astronomy, and ecclesiastical computation. As evidence of this, some of their students still survive who know Latin and Greek just as well as their native tongue" (*HE* IV.2, pp. 332–35).

It is important to realize how crucial a role such a monastery played in the civilization of England. Brief respites from habitual warfare and the acceptance of the Christian religion throughout the land could furnish but a remote occasion, a lack of hindrance, for English cultural development. The more immediate specific opportunity and cause for the development of learning was the monastery. In the ages after the Roman urban and educational systems had collapsed, when commerce and security were extremely limited, the early medieval monasteries served as oases of culture. With as few as a dozen members in their communities, they produced a sufficiency for the temporal and spiritual needs not only for themselves but for the surrounding society as well. A small core of dedicated men or women could get on nicely, separated from the stresses and demands of the outside world, producing food and shelter for the body and learning and asceticism for the soul; how-

ever, as a hardworking but unarmed community, it was vulnerable
to physical attack and an easy, tempting mark for predatory bar-
barians. Although the monastic vocation, particularly in its early
development, was antithetical to secular learning and art, it early
on had to come to terms with the necessity of that learning and
culture; for, Christian asceticism is based on the principles that God
is truth and the inspiration of all truth, that he is revealed in and
through his creation. If it was to remain true to its New Testament
legacy, in which God's Son united human flesh and divine Spirit,
it had to deal positively with the world. Furthermore, Christianity
is a religion of the book, the Bible; and the monk had to spend his
days meditating, ruminating, the words of that book. The central
activity of the monastery was always prayer, private and communal,
but it was prayer based on the Bible and the liturgy, fortified by
readings of the Fathers and the ancients. Each monk had to read or
be taught to read the Bible, the chant book, and the edifying text.

Those books, as bearers of God's message, were treated with loving
respect and decorated with the finest local art, derived from late
antique classical and, in the north, Celtic and Germanic motifs.
Music was learned and composed for the liturgy and for communal
recreation. By the eighth century the ascetical ideals of Saint Benedict's Rule and the cultural ideals of Cassiodorus's *Institutes* were
united in the continental and English monasteries. The monastic
buildings were constructed according to traditional, sometimes grand,
Roman and native models.[15] Attached to the abbey church, the
library and scriptorium, where books could be composed and copied,
were prerequisites for the school and the education of the monks.
Architecture, plastic arts, agriculture, and residential planning all
developed in the cenobitic experience. The monastery was a little
world with a special culture all its own. Because it could expand
to great numbers but also exist with very few, its culture was easily
transplanted to a new cell in a new environment, where it could
flourish independently, developing individual qualities and utilizing
native talent.

Bede's Monastery of Wearmouth-Jarrow

In the territory on the then outskirts of the known world (Britain
had been the northernmost province of the Roman Empire), a monastery was founded that proved the ideal home for a man of Bede's

genius and temperament. When Bede was born, only some seventy-five years had intervened since Augustine of Canterbury had arrived in Kent to convert the English; and only about fifty years had passed since Bede's native Northumbria had become Christian under Bishop Paulinus. But the monastery in which he grew up had developed so rapidly and richly that it had become the epitome of Christian monastic culture. Bede soon was its greatest scholar, and one of the most influential teachers of the Church in any age. Bede could be the polyhistor of his time because, in addition to his own extraordinary natural talents, in the monastery he had peace to pursue his reading, study, and teaching; and he had at his disposal one of the best libraries in Europe, assembled by the abbots of Wearmouth and Jarrow.[16]

The first and greatest abbot, Biscop, who as a monk chose the cognomen Benedict and shed his native patronymic Baducing, had been a Northumbrian noble retainer in King Oswiu's court before his decision at age twenty-five to follow a religious career. He voyaged as a pilgrim with the young Wilfrid, who was to become the controversial abbot and prelate of Hexham (and other dioceses, including York for a time) and the victor at the Council of Whitby.[17] Benedict left Wilfrid at Lyons, continued his pilgrimage to Rome and lived there before joining for two years the famed monastery of Lérins off the south coast of Gaul. He was again in Rome when Theodore was consecrated for Canterbury, and the pope sent him along to Kent as a guide for Theodore (669), where for two years he preceded Hadrian as abbot of the monastery of Saints Peter and Paul. On a third visit to the Continent and Rome he bought a large number of books, after which he returned to England to establish a new monastic community. He founded Saint Peter's at Wearmouth in 674, for which King Ecgfrith, son of Oswiu, gave a generous donation of land. Despite the prerogatives of royal patronage, Ecgfrith did not object to Benedict's obtaining a letter from Pope Agatho, exempting the monastery from all external interference. Benedict, ever the *"pius provisor"* ("loving provider") as Bede calls him, collected more books, vestments, and treasures for his monastery in his further journeys to and from Rome. On his fourth visit (third from England) he brought skilled masons and glassmakers from Gaul to build a stone church in "the Roman style that he always loved" (*HA* 5, p. 374). Anglo-Saxon secular buildings were typically wooden and relatively small, and so were the early monastic buildings at Whitby and Lindisfarne. The stone construction of Wear-mouth-Jarrow, derived from Merovingian Gaul, was monumentally extraordinary.[18] Objects not obtainable in Gaul Benedict collected in Rome on another trip; besides shipping books and relics, he transported sacred paintings on panels to adorn his church of Saint Peter: the Virgin Mary and the twelve apostles, scenes from the Gospels, and scenes from the visions of Revelation.[19] From the pope he also obtained the services of the archcantor of Saint Peter's, Abbot John, to instruct the English monks in Roman ritual and music (*HA* 6, pp. 375–76; *HE* IV.18, pp. 388–89).

A few years later (681), liking what he saw taking place at Saint Peter's, the king made another donation of land for the erection of a second monastery in the neighborhood, which Benedict established at Jarrow under the patronage of Saint Paul. Benedict transferred some twenty monks, including the boy Bede, to this new foundation under his prior, the strict and learned Ceolfrith.[20] The dedication stone of the basilica was laid 23 April 685 and is still in place. Like other seventh-century twin foundations, such as the Norman monasteries of Saint Bertin and Saint Omer and of Deux-Jumeaux and Évry (whose two houses were twenty-seven miles apart), Wearmouth and Jarrow were considered one monastery, sometimes under one abbot, sometimes under two (and during Benedict's later busy years, even under three), but always sharing the same composite rule and discipline, as established in perpetuity by their founder. As Bede wrote of them: "As the body cannot be separated from the head by which it breathes, nor the head forget the body without which it does not live, in the same manner no man should attempt by any means to divide these two monasteries, which were joined in the brotherly association of the first of the Apostles" (*HA* 7, p. 377).

Before embarking on his fifth trip to Rome, Benedict set his monastery in order "according to rule" (*HA* 6, p. 375). What is meant by rule is suggested in Chapter 11 of the *History of the Abbots*. There Bede relates that in his final injunctions to his monks, Benedict Biscop ordained that they continue to follow the rule of life compiled by him from the best ordinances of seventeen monasteries he had investigated in his many journeys; he then urged them to choose his successor according to the rule of the great abbot Benedict and in accord with their papal letter of privilege.[21] Such eclecticism was quite usual, even honored, among leaders of early monasticism. What place and extent the Rule of Saint Benedict had among the others is difficult to assess. Benedict Biscop knew the Rule of Saint Benedict from his own novitiate at Lérins, which had earlier adopted it; but he also became acquainted with the rules and customs of various monasteries in France, which had been originally founded under the rule of the Irish Saint Columban but which had absorbed the Benedictine rule as a major constituent in the direction of their communities.[22] Benedict also knew the neighboring monasteries of Wilfrid, who had chosen the Rule of Saint Benedict for his monks as their exclusive manual of discipline. Patrick Wormald has made the astute observation that "little of what we can find out about Monkwearmouth-Jarrow is actually incompatible with the Benedictine Rule," whereas Wilfrid "by contrast, whose claims to be an orthodox Benedictine are often nowadays preferred to Biscop's, ignored the rule's provisions for the succession and adopted an attitude to oblates more characteristic of Gallic than of Benedictine monasticism."[23] Wilfrid also willed property to a young relative, whereas Benedict Biscop refused to let any of his monastery's patrimony be alienated or secularized. The monastic ideals described by Bede in the *History of the Abbots* and by the author (possibly Bede) of the *Life of Ceolfrith* are those fostered in the Rule of Saint Benedict. Bede shows his familiarity with it by incorporating a number of its prescriptions and wording into his works. In addition, his description of the lives of the monks at Wearmouth-Jarrow is more in accord with the Benedictine ideal of peaceful, communal growth than with individualistic ascetic feats and pilgrimages of the Celtic tradition. These facts suggest that Benedict Biscop, who surely had taken the cognomen Benedict in admiration of the father of western monasticism, founded his *regula mixta* (composite rule) solidly on Benedict's prescripts.[24] The virtues extolled by the Benedictine rule—humility, obedience, discernment, stability, communal life, biblical and liturgical piety, ascetical moderation—are all supremely embodied in the life and writings of his most famous scion, Bede.

After appointing Eosterwine abbot of Saint Peter's, Benedict set off on his sixth trip to the Continent to acquire a supply of objects needed in his new foundation; he returned with a great treasure of books and sacred images, one series illustrating the life of Christ and another series of *figurae* depicting the concordances between the Old Testament and the New. Some part of the fabric of both churches remains (more of Saint Paul's than of Saint Peter's), but archaeological excavations have turned up none of the paintings and only a few remnants of the stained glass and decoration. Rosemary Cramp has built a model of the excavated section of the monastic buildings at Jarrow as they appeared in the eighth century; it reveals some of the extent and sophistication of this early medieval community.[25] Although the monasteries were not on the scale of those that would develop in the twelfth and following centuries at Canterbury, Cluny, and elsewhere, there were by the end of Ceolfrith's abbacy adequate facilities to house and care for six hundred monks.[26]

While Benedict Biscop provided magnificently for his abbey churches, his real ardor went to the library he had collected as the heart of his enterprise. The admirable leader's dying concern and bequest was that "the most noble and extensive library which he had brought from Rome for the necessary instruction of the church he commanded to be carefully kept entire, and neither to be injured by neglect, nor scattered about" (*HA* 11, p. 381).

His request was honored by Ceolfrith. While both he and the abbot Sigefrith (who succeeded Eosterwine at Saint Peter's) lay dying, Benedict had designated Ceolfrith abbot of both Wearmouth and Jarrow, with the full assent of the community (*HA* 13, p. 383; *Life of Ceolfrith,* 16, Plummer, I, 393–94). Ceolfrith himself, under whose direction the monastery prospered and greatly increased in size and possessions, doubled the library collection. Ceolfrith had furthered the study of the biblical text from resources that he and Benedict assembled at Wearmouth-Jarrow; he had brought from Rome a pandect (complete Bible) of the Old Latin, pre-Jerome version, *vetustae translationis,* which had belonged to Cassiodorus (*HA* 15, p. 385; *Life of Ceolfrith,* 20, Plummer, p. 395).

During Ceolfrith's abbacy the scriptorium took on some major projects, especially the "three pandects of the new translation," that is, three complete Bibles of Jerome's Vulgate version. One of these is the gorgeous Codex Amiatinus. This enormous, beautifully penned and decorated Bible, with its 1029 very large folio leaves of prime vellum written in formal uncial script by nine scribes, is accounted one of the finest books of the world, a testimony to the advanced culture of Wearmouth-Jarrow.[27] In his essay "The Scriptorium of Wearmouth-Jarrow," Malcolm Parkes has concluded that the scribal discipline demonstrated in the extant manuscripts from Wearmouth-Jarrow was a result of the excellent monastic discipline commanded by Benedict, Ceolfrith, and Ceolfrith's successor Hwætberht. Moreover, he notes, the scriptorium developed according to the monastery's special needs: since by the acquisitions of Benedict and Ceolfrith, the library already possessed a goodly collection of secondary materials and texts, and since Ceolfrith furthered biblical studies, the scribes were put to the task of writing Bibles. For this purpose they evolved a formal uncial script. Second, after Bede's death, the scribes developed a local Insular (Irish-English) miniscule handwriting to answer the enormous outside demand for works by the house author Bede.[28]

The three originating abbots of Wearmouth-Jarrow, Benedict, Eosterwine, and Ceolfrith, were of the nobility, as was usual in medieval foundations, and the first two were cousins. But Benedict was at pains to insure that following generations should rely neither on rank nor consanguinity but on virtue in selecting the head of the house. He stipulated that he would rather see the monastery leveled than that his blood brother become abbot of it (*HA* 8, p. 378; 11, p. 381; 13, p. 383). The fact that at one point in his early career as prior Ceolfrith "had to put up with the jealousies and very bitter persecution of certain men of rank, who could not brook the restraint of his conventual rule" (*Life of Ceolfrith*, 8, Boutflower, p. 60), and that he resigned and retreated to his home monastery, Wilfrid's Ripon, before being persuaded by Benedict to return, demonstrates that the leaders of the new enterprise at Wearmouth-Jarrow had to overcome class power and harmful secular attitudes. The career of Eosterwine, cut short by the plague (686), is a good example of the kind of Benedictine humility and egalitarianism the leaders inculcated and fostered in the community despite some pretty firm resistance; and it also tells us about the more mundane activities of the monastery:

Although he had been a thegn of King Ecgfrith's, when once he had abandoned the affairs of the world and laid arms aside, and had taken upon himself the warfare of the spirit, he remained so humble and so wholly like the other brethren that he rejoiced to thresh and winnow with them, to milk ewes and cows and to be employed in the bakehouse, the garden, and the kitchen; and in all the labors of the monastery, he was cheerful and obedient. When he attained the power and rank of abbot, he retained the same attitude as before toward everybody. . . . Often, when he went out anywhere to see to the business of the monastery, if he found brethren working, he would quickly join them in their task by taking the plow handle to direct its course, or by subduing iron with the smith's hammer, or by shaking the winnowing fan with his hand, or by

doing anything of that kind. For he was a young man of great strength
and pleasant speech, cheerful in spirit, generous in giving, and of distinguished appearance. He ate the same food as the other brethren, and always
in the same room. He slept in the same common room as he did before
he was abbot, so that even after he was taken ill and already saw his death
by clear signs, he still lay for two days in the dormitory of the brethren
(*HA* 8, p. 378).[29]

Bede's Life, Learning, and Works

In this dynamic and disciplined monastery Bede passed his life.
As Gregory of Tours affixed a short autobiography to the end of his
History of the Franks (X.31; written between 584 and 591), Bede
appended to his *Ecclesiastical History* a brief curriculum vitae with a
bibliography of his works to date (731). There he relates most of
the details of his quiet, scholarly religious life that we have. Elsewhere, even in his letters and the history of his abbots, he rarely
speaks of himself. All other biographical information must be extracted from such sources as Cuthbert's letter about Bede's death,
from occasional mentions of Bede and his legacy by disciples and
admirers, such as Alcuin and Boniface, and from inferences and
oblique references in his own and other authors' writings. There is
no early life of Bede; those extant were all composed at least four
hundred years after his death. Except for the details of his death,
the only contemporary account is his own. This is what he says:

I, Bede, servant of Christ and priest of the monastery of St. Peter and St.
Paul which is at Wearmouth and Jarrow, have, with the help of God and
to the best of my ability, put together this account of the history of the
Church of Britain and of the English people in particular, gleaned either
from ancient documents or from tradition or from my own knowledge. I
was born in the territory of this monastery. When I was seven years of
age I was, by the care of my kinsmen, put into the charge of the reverend
Abbot Benedict and then of Ceolfrith, to be educated. From then on I
have spent all my life in this monastery, applying myself entirely to the
study of Scriptures; and, amid the observance of the discipline of the Rule
and the daily task of singing in the church, it has always been my delight
to learn or to teach or to write. At the age of nineteen I was ordained
deacon and at the age of thirty, priest, both times through the ministration
of the reverend Bishop John on the direction of Abbot Ceolfrith. From
the time I became a priest until the fifty-ninth year of my life I have made
it my business, for my own benefit and that of my brothers, to make brief

extracts from the works of the venerable fathers on the holy Scriptures, or to add notes of my own to clarify their sense and interpretation (*HE* V.24, p. 567).

In the early manuscripts of the *History* and in other contemporary sources his name appears as Bæda, which no doubt the author answered to; in the Middle Ages he was Beda, but to English-speaking people he is known as Bede. His native name, like that of the abbot Biscop Baducing, is uncommon;[30] unlike Biscop, who took the name Benedict in religion, Bede did not have a cognomen. His ancestry is unknown; like the priest Melchizedek in the Book of Genesis (14:18), "he has no father, mother, or ancestry" (Heb. 7:1). Henry Mayr-Harting suggests that with his clerical ideal of a classless monastic society Bede deliberately suppressed biographical data of family and parentage, linking himself closely only to his monastery.[31] Since he speaks of being in the care of kinsmen *(cura propinquorum)* as a child, some have assumed that he was an orphan, but without any further evidence. He does not speak of his rank or kinship, as he does in cases of many of the monks and abbots he wrote about. Despite his eminent authority in later life, Bede was never selected to be prior or abbot; perhaps his social status hindered his having to take on a burden that would have impaired his real contribution to history as a writer. For, even though Benedict Biscop, following the rule of Saint Benedict, urged the selection of the best man for the position of abbot irrespective of birth, de facto all the early abbots of Wearmouth-Jarrow were nobles. This is also true of other English monasteries of the era, such as Hild's Whitby, Aldhelm's Malmesbury, and Wilfrid's Hexham.

Bede was born fittingly on land that a year or two later (674) became the monastery's domain. Bede spoke highly of localities sacred to Christianity, such as the Holy Land (for which he wrote a guidebook), Rome, and Canterbury; and he praised the Roman pilgrimage efforts of kings, such as Oswiu and Cædwalla, and of monks, such as Benedict Biscop and Ceolfrith, as "acts of great merit" (see *HE* IV.23, p. 409). Nonetheless, except for a few short trips (we know of one to Lindisfarne and one to York), he never engaged in the kind of pilgrimage beloved by Celtic and Irish-trained monks. He spent the rest of his life in his monastery. Truly he practiced the Benedictine virtue of stability.[32]

Although many in the community, like his superiors Benedict

and Ceolfrith, had entered religion as adults, Bede was put into the monastery to be educated at age seven. In the early Middle Ages oblates entered the cloister as early as age five.[33] Parallel to this custom of enrolling a child in the monastery, there also existed among the English and other Germanic peoples a secular tradition of fosterage, whereby at age seven a promising boy was placed in the court of a prince or noble for proper training (there are many instances of such a practice, from Beowulf to Chaucer). Thus, there were both religious and secular precedents for Bede's fosterage. Bede says that he was first put under Benedict Biscop but then afterwards under Ceolfrith. Bede does not say when he was transferred from Wearmouth to Jarrow, but since he does not speak of serving under Eosterwine, abbot of Saint Peter's, Bede was probably in that first select group to enter the new monastery of Jarrow under Ceolfrith.

Whenever pestilence broke out in England, the monasteries were hit particularly hard, because of their communal life and fraternal assistance. In 685–86, with Benedict away on his sixth journey to Rome, disease wiped out many monks at Wearmouth, including the abbot Eosterwine, and, according to the anonymous *Life of Ceolfrith,* chapter 14, at Jarrow all the choir monks with the exception of Ceolfrith and a little boy under his instruction. The abbot decided, as the Rule of Benedict directs for such circumstances (17.3), that the two of them should dispense with chanting the antiphons to the psalms of the Little Hours of the Office, but after a week they could bear it no longer and restored the antiphons.[34] They made do with untrained brothers until a sufficient number of new singers could be educated. Since Bede would have been about twelve at the time, many historians, following Plummer, have assumed that the boy referred to in this touching story of monastic devotion to psalmody was Bede. That is possible, but it may have been some other boy, such as Hwætberht, who was also about twelve at the time, or even the anonymous author himself of the *Life of Ceolfrith* (if that is not Bede also).[35] Even if the little boy was not Bede, it gives a glimpse into the character of his prime mentor, whose "incomparable conscientiousness in praying and singing the psalms" he lauded (*HA* 16, p. 386). Bede was a great admirer of Ceolfrith, and as an adult was so strongly moved by Ceolfrith's demise that he could not work for a time (preface, *In I Samuhelis* IV, CCSL 119, p. 212).

Bede's early education was obviously successful. As part of his earliest training in singing the psalms in choir, he learned chant, which had been inculcated at Wearmouth-Jarrow by the Roman archcantor John. He was thoroughly grounded in piety and ascetical training, in the liturgy, prayer, and the devout life. These elements are prominent in all his work, and his religious idealism persisted throughout his career. His piety was as noted as his learning. Alcuin, who thought of Bede as his own *magister,* wrote to the monks of Wearmouth-Jarrow: "It is reported that our master and your patron, blessed Bede, said, 'I know that angels visit the canonical hours and the fraternal congregations; what if they do not find me there among the brothers? Will they not have to say, "Where is Bede? Why has he not come to the appointed prayers with his brothers?" ' "[36]

The usual monastic day, after the prescribed seven hours of the office in choir *(opus Dei),* allocated some four hours for reading and studying, and, depending on the season, some five to seven hours for work. Since even abbots like Eosterwine and Hwætberht did menial work in the monastery (*HA* 8, pp. 377–78), the young monk Bede must certainly have had to perform domestic duties. In the increasingly active scriptorium Bede would have to do his stints, learning various scripts and styles; as he later remarked to Bishop Acca with a quiet note of irony, his training in writing, copying, and shorthand served him in good stead since he had to do all his writing without secretarial assistance: "ipse mihi dictator simul notarius et librarius existerem" (prologus, *In Lucam,* CCSL 120, p. 7). Apparently, only during his last days did he have an amanuensis. Study at first involved the basics of grammar and pronunciation in preparation of the correct performance of the liturgy, and the memorization of psalms. Later, the reading of Latin texts, orthography, punctuation, accent, and translation followed. Bede was able from late antique grammar texts and classical and postclassical authors to learn his Latin well for its use in the liturgy, the office and mass, and for reading and expounding the Bible, commentaries, works of the Fathers, and history. In Bede's time, grammar, which embraced both the rules for correct reading and writing and the interpretation and analysis of texts, was the fundamental discipline of a young monk's education. Already in the late antique period, the classical subject of rhetoric had been subsumed in large part into the interpretative elements of grammar, and dialectic (logic) had largely disappeared as a scholastic subject. Moreover, rhetoric as an educational tool was under a religious cloud because it purported to persuade without regard to actual fact, to move the mind and heart by clever and beautiful art, not by truth. There is reason to believe that Bede knew some basic rhetorical treatises, but he was always discreet in his application of them and never admitted to them as part of his intellectual formation. Grammar, however, figured in his life and works prominently, especially in the art of scriptural exegesis. It also aided him in his poetic studies, so important for liturgical hymnology and hagiography, since its broad compass included metrics and scansion.

For an understanding of his biblical and ecclesiastical world, he learned some fundamental lore about nature, astronomy, and, particularly for the determining of the ecclesiastical calendar, computation. In computation and chronology Bede became the master of his age.

Bede's training in monastic arts and letters was extensive and appreciative. Judging from his remarks in the commentaries in defense of pictorial images (*De templo,* CCSL 119A, pp. 212–13, 808–44; *Octo quaestionum liber* II, PL 93.456), Bede was deeply and favorably impressed by religious art, such as he saw in the church and manuscripts imported by Benedict Biscop.[37] His early studies were directed to the eventual goal of maturely understanding, contemplating, and correctly interpreting the word of God in the Bible. His training instilled in him the Augustinian conviction pervasive in all his writings, especially the early educational ones, that the Bible is "the standard of all literacy and exegesis the central problem of all learning."[38] The historical discipleship of Christ through the ages, the working out of the Christian's life after Jesus, spurred Bede's study in hagiology and eventually his career as a hagiographer as well as exegete.

The only teacher besides Ceolfrith Bede mentions by name is Tunberht, trained under Chad at Lastingham, who taught Bede the Scriptures (*HE* IV.3, pp. 342–43). It is clear from Bede's own works and the reputation for vast learning that he enjoyed in his lifetime and after that he rapidly outgrew and surpassed his instructors and many of the textbooks. Although as a rule Bede sedulously avoided outspoken criticism of any authority, especially religious, the fact that he found it necessary to spend most of his lifetime furnishing good or improved texts to students indicates the deficiencies in the texts he himself as a student originally had to work with.

He must very soon have been outstanding, both as a scholar and as a monk, for he tells us himself (*HE* V.24, pp. 566–67) that he was ordained deacon at the age of nineteen, six years before the canonical age. Exceptions were occasionally made in the case of other men of outstanding learning and devotion also, but the fact that the canonical age was anticipated by six years bears witness to the esteem in which he was held by Ceolfrith. It was the latter who was responsible for presenting him to Bishop John of Hexham, better known as Saint John of Beverley, of whom Bede speaks lovingly in the early chapters of his fifth book (*HE* V.2–6, pp. 456–69). Bede was ordained priest in 703, and the rest of his life was that of a scholar-monk (Colgrave, *HE,* pp. xx–xxi).

When Ceolfrith appointed Bede as the master of education at Saint Paul's we do not know. Probably before his ordination he taught at least the first two of the three basic disciplines of grammar, computus, and music: grammar to understand the word of Scripture; computus, the study of liturgical time (not only for the proper dating of Easter but because monastic ascesis "was regulated from bell-stroke to forever" (Jones, introduction, CCSL 118A, p. vi); and music, because the *opus Dei* was performed as chant in complex modes. For these disciplines, except for music (if we exclude metrics and hymns), Bede composed a number of texts. The learned editor of Bede's *Opera didascalia* thinks it probable that Bede was also the choirmaster in his monastery (the choirmaster at least in some Benedictine houses was both teacher and librarian).[39] That may well be so, but the fact that Bede speaks of his daily duty as singer in the church does not confirm the supposition. A more convincing bit of evidence is the remark made by Cuthbert in his Letter on the Death of Bede, that links Bede's daily instructing with chant performance: "He desired to finish two little works worthy of record, besides the lessons which we received from him daily and the singing of the Psalms" (Colgrave and Mynors, *HE,* pp. 582–83). If Bede instructed in music practice, he had no means of writing a practical text for it, since there was no system of writing notation until much later (Augustine's and Boethius's theoretical tracts *De musica* could serve no instructional purpose for the singing of Gregorian chant).

Bede did write texts as part of grammatical instruction on metrics and figurative language, and he organized a handbook on correct usage. He did a small piece on natural science, and two major works, one early and the other late and completely revised, on computus, that is, instruction in the complicated science of time reckoning. Throughout his lifetime Bede proved that he could expertly do himself what he taught in class. He wrote a book of hymns in various meters, a book (now lost) of poetic epigrams, and occasional poems. He composed a versified and a prose *Life of St. Cuthbert* as well as other saints' lives and a martyrology.

As a mature priest-scholar Bede produced commentaries on books of the Old and New Testament, by far the largest section of his collected works. Many of these commentaries consist of arranged and edited borrowings from the works of prominent Fathers of the Church, especially of the four western Fathers, Ambrose, Augustine, Jerome, and Gregory the Great. In his prefaces Bede regularly informs his readers of his principal sources. Contrary to the usual medieval practice, he often gives specific citations in the text, and, in the case of his commentaries on Mark and Luke, in the margin. He summarizes his authorities, lucidly and accurately, in addition to supplying his own reading of a text not treated to his satisfaction by an earlier author. Bede shows a concern for the accuracy of the text and sometimes questions whether scribes have copied a text faithfully. He is concerned about the problem of dealing with translated texts of the Bible, from Hebrew or Greek into a variety of Latin versions. "His interest in the text criticism of the Bible was unique in his age," notes M. L. W. Laistner.[40] Despite their eclectic nature, Bede's biblical treatises gained an enormous popularity and established Bede as a doctor of the Church, ranked with the Fathers by admiring generations of medieval commentators. Bede had no wish to be original, a quality authors and public have seen as praiseworthy since the nineteenth century; rather, he wished as he often said "to follow the footsteps of the Fathers" in bringing the truth of the Scriptures and its interpreters to a dark age. No doubt Abbot Ceolfrith's own biblical interests served as a guide and support. Always scrupulous of the truth and vehemently opposed to heresy, Bede strove to convey the deepest meaning of the text by way of intelligent interpretation. That interpretation was often allegorical, that is, stressing the deeper religious sense and significance of an historic or literal event. Since Bede is concerned with providing interpretations that are pertinent to monastic asceticism, he favors and constructs commentary that is personally applicable, spiritual, and mystical (in the sense of aiming for the union of the individual soul with God).[41]

Bede began his exegetical exercises on books of the New Testament; in later life he concentrated on the Old Testament. Some of the books he tackled had not been commented on directly by earlier Fathers and theologians. His purposes were therefore either to furnish traditional commentary derived from established sources but put in a simplified form for his English students or to fill for them the gaps in which no commentary yet existed. Although he learned some Greek early in his career, he took great pains to gain a better mastery of it for his later work, and as a result published a revised version of his commentary on the Acts of the Apostles based on his careful readings of the Greek text.

Among the theological works for which he was well known in the Middle Ages are the two books of homilies, containing fifty reflections on the Gospels, many excerpted from his gospel commentaries. These homilies found their way into homiletic collections for the use of preachers during the course of the ecclesiastical year. Soon after Bede's life, many of the sermons were truncated, augmented, or otherwise rearranged.

Although Bede was honored in the Middle Ages mainly for his theological treatises, he is best known to our age as an historian. The accomplishment of the *Ecclesiastical History of the English Nation* gained Bede the accolade of "father of English history," and the uniquely valuable information it furnishes puts all English, medieval, and church historians greatly in his debt. It is also a masterpiece of literature, and its early translation into Old English (at the end of the ninth century) further enhances its worth for literary historians. Bede's *History of the Abbots of Wearmouth and Jarrow,* though much more limited in its scope and length, is also an important study, for it presents the lives and careers of the first abbots of Wearmouth-Jarrow under whom Bede served, and it describes the life and spirit of the monastery itself.

For this work he mined all the sources available to him; these were considerable because of the extensive library of Wearmouth-Jarrow and the practice of borrowing works from other ecclesiastical establishments (the monastic equivalent of interlibrary loan), as well as personal exchange and correspondence. Fifty years ago Laistner, despite his expertise in Bedan manuscripts and writings but having for the most part only the badly edited texts by Giles and the *Patrologia Latina* to work with, tentatively catalogued the library of Bede from references and traces left in his writings; these amounted

to some 150 titles by 75 authors, as well as various versions of the
Bible. Laistner did not include important hagiographical sources
known to Bede, and since 1935 modern Bedan editors and other
scholars have found evidence for a good many more sources, some
obscure (such as Velius Longus) but some quite obvious and familiar
to us (such as *The Rule of Saint Benedict*).[42] Tracing documentable
sources in Bede's works can produce misleading results, because like
any scholar Bede did not identifiably record in his writings everything he read, and some of the writings he got secondhand (this is
particularly true of grammatical sources, which notoriously incorporate previous authors' examples and rules). Nevertheless, such a
list suggests the kind and number of materials Bede had available,
and from the perspective of the eighth century, his resources were
extraordinary, his reading and assimilation vast.

He acknowledged his debt to the resolute book collecting of
Benedict Biscop and Ceolfrith. In his memorial sermon for Benedict,
Bede noted that as often as the founder went abroad he brought
back a great supply of holy books and other materials, so that his
sons would be be freed from want and abound in spiritual resources
(*Hom.* I.13, CCSL 122, pp. 92–93). He speaks with satisfaction
about Ceolfrith's doubling the collection (*HA* 15, p. 385). He writes
letters and prefaces to thank benefactors for books and informants
for important information. Most of all he searched for knowledge
in the Scriptures, the Fathers, the histories, and the lives. As a good
scholar, Bede plundered the past to enlighten the present; as a good
thinker, he arranged his sources well, adding his own contributions;
as a good writer, he presented his material in a lucid, soberly elegant
style.

During his productive life Bede wrote some important letters that
have been preserved. He lists five of them in his bibliography at
the end of the *History*. Another two date from his last years: a brief
letter to Albinus, abbot of the monastery of Saints Peter and Paul
at Canterbury to accompany a copy of the *History;* and the famous
outspoken epistle to Ecgberht on the critical state of the Church in
Northumbria.

How was Bede able to generate so great a corpus (twelve volumes
in Giles's edition) on topics of nearly every subject in the monastic
curriculum? He was a quietly productive worker of genius and
assiduity, who understood the urgent need for his contribution to

his community, church, and people. Despite his constantly other-
worldly outlook, he tells us that he enjoyed his teaching and writing.

Bede died as he lived, teaching and praying. Bede's disciple
Cuthbert, afterwards abbot of Wearmouth-Jarrow, wrote a letter
describing Bede's last days. He remarks, "I never saw or heard of
any man so diligent in returning thanks to the living God," and
he adds that Bede, "learned in our songs," used to repeat a grim
little Old English religious poem about preparedness for passing
and judgment.[43] The letter tells how beautifully prepared he was
(*HE,* pp. 580–81). He did not simply languish: he continued to
give lessons from his bed, to translate the Gospel of John (1:1–6:9)
into English, and to make certain corrections in Isidore's book *On
the Wonders of Nature* because, he said, "I cannot have my children
learning a lie and losing labor on this after my passing" (pp. 582–
83).[44] On the very day of his death he dictated a chapter of a book.
That evening he disposed of a few small gifts to the brothers[45] and
expressed to them the sentiment, "My soul longs to see Christ my
King in all his beauty." The young scribe Wilberht said: " 'There
is still one sentence, dear master, not written down.' And he said,
'Write it.' After a little the boy said: 'There, now it is written.'
And he replied: 'Good. It is finished (John 19:30); you have spoken
the truth.' And so upon the floor of his cell, singing 'Glory be to
the Father and to the Son and to the Holy Spirit' and the rest, he
breathed his last" (Cuthbert's Letter, *HE,* pp. 584–85).

Chapter Two
The Educational Treatises

Through the civilization the Christian Church brought to the British Isles, the fundamental Roman educational system, which had been appropriated from the Greeks and reduced to prescription, served to train the native clergy. The Roman program consisted almost entirely in the study of letters, which well suited ecclesiastic needs. The seven liberal arts, made up of the trivium (grammar, rhetoric, dialectic) and of the quadrivium (arithmetic, geometry, music, astronomy) theoretically constituted classical education. They were celebrated as a unity in Martianus Capella's allegorical treatise, *The Marriage of Philology and Mercury* (c. 410–27); Cassiodorus, former minister of Theodoric and then founder of the humanistic monastery Vivarium, made them the basis of his exposition of secular learning in his *Divine and Secular Readings;* Isidore devotes a paragraph to them in the *Etymologies* (I.2). Nonetheless, de facto education of the late antique and early medieval periods consisted of two disciplines, grammar and rhetoric, and sometimes only grammar in an expanded format, which brought in the other subjects as props and adjunct information. Bede makes no mention of the seven liberal arts.

The Roman Educational Legacy

Each of the four great Fathers of the western Church, Ambrose, Augustine, Jerome, and Gregory, whose footsteps Bede strove to follow, had received an aristocratic Roman education in letters before their religious careers.[1] The goal of that education had originally been the formation of the citizen-statesman, and therefore it emphasized the acquisition of linguistic skills through the disciplines of grammar and rhetoric, with some borrowings from dialectic for argumentation and persuasion. The material that served as the norm of excellence and supplied the examples for the study of grammar and rhetoric was classical Latin literature—poetry, history, and oratory. In the late antique period, teachers used handbooks with the literary examples extracted and classified according to topic, so that pupils first knew the classics at a remove from their original context, surrounded by pedantic commentary. Like so much else in the nostalgic years of the crumbling Roman Empire education was extremely conservative and formalized.

To understand the tradition that Bede the grammarian received, a few details about the earlier Roman educational system are necessary.[2] Between the ages of seven and twelve a boy would be given elementary instruction in reading, writing, and calculation by a primary teacher. Then the grammarian would take over the child's instruction, teaching him to speak and write with style, and to become acquainted with classical authors. The grammarian's task was therefore twofold: to teach the art of writing and speaking correctly, and then the art of interpreting the text. The first part of the grammarian's charge was not easy even when teaching native speakers of Latin, for their Latin had undergone considerable mutations from the classical form the grammarian championed. As Latin developed from its classical past to its medieval forms, it was necessary for the grammarian to place special emphasis on correct spelling and usage (the discipline of orthography), in order to avoid innovations carried over from the spoken language. Teaching the basics to pupils whose native speech was Germanic, such as the English, by a grammarian who knew late rather than classical Latin was doubly hard. The grammarian also had the responsibility of teaching prosody and metrics, so that the student might learn proper prose cadences and read and compose poetry according to classical norms, again made the more difficult by changes in pronunciation of the language. The loss of differentiation of the quantitative length or brevity of vowels and syllables further obfuscated the essence of classical poetry. On his part the student was called upon to do grammatical and writing exercises, to read and write sample passages with correct accent and punctuation, to transpose short poems into prose, and to paraphrase moral maxims. The second part of the grammarian's mandate, the explication of the classics to the child, was fulfilled by devoting hours to verse-by-verse, line-by-line exegesis of a text. This involved both grammatical analysis and elucidation of the meaning by calling upon encyclopedic lore from history, law, and science.

For all this, school texts were needed. Basic grammatical texts, descended from Greek Stoic and Alexandrian treatises, furnished a schematic analysis of language.[3] Jerome's respected teacher, Donatus, whose name was synonymous with grammar for Gregory as for generations afterwards, provided the best-known grammatical texts; these served as the bases for many of Bede's grammatical treatises. The *Ars minor* of Donatus is a short treatise on the eight parts of speech; his more extensive *Ars grammatica (maior)* deals with (1) the articulated components of language (sound, syllable, feet, tone, pauses), (2) the parts of speech, and (3) literary virtues and vices (metaplasms, figures, and tropes; barbarisms, solecisms, other faults) (Keil, 4:355–402). Priscian's *Institutio de nomine et pronomine et uerbo (Instruction about the Noun, Pronoun, and Verb)* supplemented Donatus's treatment of inflectional parts of speech, and along with Isidore of Seville's first book of the *Etymologies* (On Grammar and Its Parts) formed with Donatus the core of the English grammarian's library. There existed a score of other textbooks by authors such as Charisius, Diomedes, Sacerdos, Maximus Victorinus, Probus, Consentius, Asper, and Augustine. They all attemped much the same thing. Typically they included three main divisions: the study of (1) sound, with letter and syllable; (2) the eight parts of speech; (3) the virtues and vices of speech, that is, good and bad usage, including stylistic devices. One class of these grammars offered the basic materials, with slight variations; the other class presented expanded versions, with more sophisticated treatments.

In the Roman tradition, if a young man around age sixteen wished to become polished and proficient, he presented himself to the rhetor, who instructed him in the fine art of persuasion. The rhetor taught the oratorical rules and devices, how to discover and explore the commonplaces *(topoi),* how to create a speech from exordium through its development and argumentation to the peroration, and finally, how to deliver the speech effectively. Rhetoric was a study of rules and examples that treated much of the same material that grammar had over the years appropriated from rhetoric, but in a more elaborate way. From great speakers and writers the student amassed a supply of sayings and techniques that he was to utilize in standard exercises in eulogy, description, and moral theme. He had to compose and deliver fictitious speeches, which were framed as either controversial cases or suasive deliberations on some topic from history or myth. In his rhetorical training, just as he borrowed from grammar the techniques of language, he also learned from dialectic how to make logical arguments and clever debate, even though the science of dialectic itself no longer constituted a separate discipline.

After years of training in rhetoric, at about twenty-one, the young man could enter a career as teacher, lecturer, or, after some legal apprenticeship, lawyer. Ambrose and Gregory became civil administrators, Augustine and Paulinus of Nola, teachers of rhetoric. Augustine's *Confessions* presents a marvelous personal account of a late antique career developing from rudiments through grammar and rhetoric to fame and success as rhetor in Carthage, Rome, and Milan.

Each of these great men, products of late Roman education, rejected pagan secular tradition and their training in it when they turned wholly to the Christian life. Jerome's own rhetorical and dialectical powers were extraordinary and his diatribes and controversial works venomously potent. Yet he repudiated those very developed gifts in his famous Letter 22, in which he reports the numbing vision of Christ accusing him of being a Ciceronian and not a Christian.[4] In the *Confessions* Augustine remarks how terrible it was that literary artifice could make him in his youth weep for Dido's dereliction by Aeneas but not for his own sins.[5] In a famous statement to Desiderius Gregory refused to submit to the rules of grammar because he thought it "highly improper to subject the words of the celestial oracle to the rules of Donatus. None of the interpreters have observed these rules in regard to the authority of sacred Scripture."[6] Ambrose had made the same point.[7] Gregory was also scandalized by the report that Bishop Desiderius of Vienne was teaching grammar, since that entailed the teaching of profane literature; Gregory insisted that "the same mouth cannot utter the praises of both Jupiter and Christ."[8]

Nevertheless, the Fathers recognized that secular studies were necessary requisites for the reading of Scripture; they had to admit the worth of them in their own lives as exegetes. Each recognized the debt owed to his education in preparing him to understand and interpret the great text, the Bible. Jerome asserted that profane literature could be a useful assistant just as the beautiful captive woman in Deuteronomy (21:11–13) could become a good Jewish wife.[9] Similarly, Augustine tolerated profane studies if appropriated to the study of the sacred text: "History helps us a great deal in the understanding of sacred books, even if we learn it outside of

the Church as part of our childhood education." On the analogy of
the Israelites despoiling the treasures of the Egyptians by divine
command (Exod. 3:22; 11:2; 12:55), Augustine argued that Christians ought to feel free to expropriate from pagan literature "the
liberal disciplines more suited to the uses of truth."[10] Gregory said,
"In knowing the liberal arts we understand divine words better."
For that reason only, the study of profane literature was allowed.[11]

In an unrefined view, the Fathers had a love-hate relationship
with their civilization and were ambivalent about the use of classical
letters in the Christian community. But upon a more sensitive
reading, we see that they distinguished, not always carefully, between the illegitimate indulgence in the reading and enjoyment of
pagan literature and the pragmatic appreciation of pagan letters for
educating the Christian to read and enjoy Scripture sophisticatedly
and to defend the Christian position against the subtle attacks of
erudite enemies. As to the actual use of classical literature and
rhetoric in their works, Jerome is on one end of the spectrum with
the fullest usage and Gregory on the other with the least; but all
the Fathers draw upon their classical training and repertoire. It is
also important to remember that, whether rejected or not, the values
and attitudes culled from Roman education pervaded the Fathers'
thought, and as a result much that filtered through the system as
Catholic doctrine about history, society, sexuality, and morality was
Roman and not specifically Christian.

Grammar in the Monastic Curriculum

That was the situation in the fifth and sixth centuries: except for
isolated and abortive enterprises such as Cassiodorus's Vivarium,
there was little education except profane education; and that had to
be grudgingly accepted if Christians were to be literate and develop
their religion within the Roman milieu. The four Fathers of the
Church had already received their secular education by the time
they examined it in their religious maturity. The situation became
radically different in the age of monasticism, for then all education
had to meet the need and ideal of the religious life. Monastic rules
of the West made but one scholastic demand: literacy. Grammar
was welcomed and fostered in the monastery because it provided
this indispensable skill as well as the interpretative methods necessary for the communal and personal perusal of the Bible and holy

books. Rhetoric and dialectic, however, with their goals of artful argument and cunning suasion, could only be permitted, if at all, under considerable strictures. In later Benedictine tradition, classically described by Jean Leclercq, the more humane love of learning with studies in the arts could in some centers be coupled with the pursuit of virtue.[12] Wearmouth-Jarrow under its first abbots was more rigorous in its interpretation.

Some of the English may have been imbued with Anglo-Saxon aristocratic secular values when they turned, like Benedict Biscop and Ceolfrith, to religion. Certain prelates who had lived at court in their youth, such as Aldhelm (c. 639–709/10), enjoyed reputations as native poets, *scops*. Their education in letters, however, was monastic and Latinate. Monks who, like Bede and Hwætberht, entered the monastery as children had scarcely the opportunity to participate in the Anglo-Saxon secular code. In Bede's day, there was no secular education in letters, indeed there was no formal education at all outside the Church—the monastery and, to a lesser extent, the cathedral school. The monk was to be trained in the service of the Lord, though some, like Benedict Biscop, were called upon for service to the state by the secular lord.[13] In any case, there was no apparent reason why the monastic curriculum should provide anything more than the study of grammar (for the reading of the Bible and liturgy and composition of hagiography, history, and hymns, and for the correct writing of manuscripts), computus (for the reckoning of the church calendar and history), and the practical arts of music performance (for chanting the texts of office and the mass), as well as physical arts such as husbandry, agriculture, and domestic management.

As the science that teaches one how to persuade and sway an audience regardless of the truth or falsity of one's position (indeed, the shakier the case, the greater should be the rhetoric to compensate for its weakness), rhetoric was held suspect. But Scripture often presents examples of what are called rhetorical devices, and knowledge of those devices was needed to understand the pregnant meaning of the text. Because grammar had already usurped large parts of rhetoric's subject, such as rhythm, metrics, figures of speech,[14] the curriculum at Wearmouth-Jarrow could safely dispense with a formal course in rhetoric and could teach the expanded discipline of grammar to cover the literary bases. There is no evidence that either a course in rhetoric was taught at Wearmouth-Jarrow or that rhetoric texts, such as Quintilian's or the anonymous *Ad Herennium* were in the Wearmouth-Jarrow library.[15]

Bede's own attitude towards Roman rhetoric was, from the evidence of his textbooks and commentaries, ambivalent and in some instances strongly antagonistic. Like the Fathers he recognizes that rhetorical artifice can be most alluring, that in the hands of heretics or the devil it can lead astray and entice to evil. For example, speaking of the wanton woman in chapter 7 of Proverbs as a figure of heresy, he remarks that the description of her bed's coverlet with its decorated Egyptian tapestry signifies "the adornment of eloquence and the trickery of dialectical art, which took its origin from the pagans."[16] Bede has harsh things to say about philosophers: "A certain one of ours nicely remarked that philosophers are the patriarchs of heretics."[17] Philosophers, of course, had been identified with sophists and dialecticians since antiquity. Elsewhere, explicating a text about the hostile Samaritans' eating salted food in the palace of Artaxerxes, Bede explains that they were thus corrupted "by the taste of worldly philosophy, by the sweetness of rhetoric, and by the trickery of dialectical art."[18] He excoriates those contemporaries who should ascend to hearing the word of God but instead descend to listen to "secular fables and teachings of demons, reading the dialecticians, rhetoricians, and poets of the gentiles."[19] Indeed, Bede strongly discouraged the reading of pagan literature. In *De arte metrica* he mentions a volume by the poet Porphyry cited by Jerome that exemplifies various meters, but adds: "Because they were pagan, it was not permitted for us to touch them."[20] Nevertheless, though he prefers to quote Christian poets whenever possible, Bede does plunder the pagans, particularly Virgil, and points out that there is precedent in Moses's learning all the wisdom of the Egyptians, Daniel's learning the language and culture of the Chaldaeans, and Paul's quoting Greek poets.[21]

As a monastic educator, Bede expresses strong reservations about rhetoric and dialectic; but that does not mean that he did not know the basics of rhetoric nor believe that in the hands of a qualified, mature scholar it could serve a useful purpose. As Roger Ray has demonstrated, a key text that reveals Bede's positive attitude towards the subject is in book II of his commentary on I Samuel.[22] After warning that Christians should neither love nor pursue too ardently the sweetness of secular eloquence, he discusses the meaning of Jonathan's nourishment from the forbidden honeycomb. Certain noble leaders of the Church enjoyed the books of the pagans too much, and one of them was severely chastised for being a Ciceroninan rather than a Christian (here Bede means Jerome, of course). Yet Jonathan's eyes were brightened by the honey, and so the properly careful wise one instructed in the doctrine of the Church and in letters can say: "I have become more effective, acute, and ready to speak what are fitting, in so far as I have tasted a little from the flower of the Tullian text (CCSL 119, pp. 120–21). The use of the phrase *Tullianae lectionis* implies some approbation of Ciceronian rhetoric. Texts such as these counterbalance those that seem to deplore the use of classical sources and rhetoric. Nonetheless, in practice Bede seems to align himself more closely with Gregory's attitudes than with any of the other Fathers; he prefers to cite Christian authors, except for Virgil, and leaves very few, if any, identifiable traces of classical rhetoric.

In the abbey school the two main disciplines were grammar and biblical exegesis, with some study of time reckoning and a bit of natural history and geography as a complement to the Bible. Bede made texts for each of these. As in all his work he aimed for a clear, easily understandable presentation of the principles and details of the curricular subjects. Unlike Boniface and Alcuin of the next generation, Bede did not compose a new type of grammar for teaching Latin to his Germanic learners. Donatus was deemed generally adequate for his purposes, and the library of Wearmouth-Jarrow, like most other English monasteries, possessed such a text; it boasted an admirable collection of other grammatical treatises as well. Where he did find Donatus inadequate was in the treatment of metrics and figures of speech.[23]

Bede's Grammatical Works

At the end of the *Historia ecclesiastica* Bede gives a bibliography of his writings. Among them is "a book on the art of meter" (*HE* V.24, pp. 570–71). This *De arte metrica* (CCSL 123A, pp. 81–141) is a systematic exposition of Latin versification by means of a judicious compilation of grammarians' commentaries on Donatus (principally Servius's continuation, *De finalibus,* of Donatus's *De pedibus,* with excerpts from Pompeius, Sergius, Audax, and others), replete with examples from Virgil and Christian poets. Because it contains a reasonably full account of most Latin classical and post-

classical metrical usage, the little treatise could instruct a pupil who
had laid the foundation of Latin grammar in earlier studies how to
recognize and read correctly the verse forms found in hymns, metrical saints' lives, epigrams, the liturgical chants, as well as in
classical Latin poetry. Although the piece is mainly a compilation
of extracts, Bede's careful arrangement and presentation of the material made it a standard, even indispensable text in the age of
Charlemagne. Bede's excellence as a textbook writer emerges from
a comparison with the texts of the grammarians he cites, from his
order of selection, his omission of nonessential material and editing
of the rest, the accuracy, simplicity, and precision of his definitions,
and the formation of a new synthesis that respects the authority of
his sources.[24] He discusses without digression what the letters are,
their classifications and characteristics (chap. 1), then proceeds to
syllables (chaps. 2–8) and to feet (chap. 9) before the treatment on
metrics (chaps. 10–23), rhythm (chap. 24), and the three genres
of poetry. That Bede does not slavishly follow his grammatical
sources but modifies his definitions according to his own observations is apparent in chapters 16–22 but especially in chapter 23,
on trochaic tetrameter (CCSL 123A, pp. 137–38), where he makes
several alterations in the statements of his source, Mallius Theodorus
(consul, A.D. 399), in order to describe more accurately actual early
medieval poetic practice, specifically in the hymn he cites as an
example.[25] Bede's major contribution to metrical history is his original description in chapter 24 of isosyllabic stress rhythm (that is,
accentual meter), which superseded quantitative Latin verse in medieval poetry.

     In an epilogue, Bede dedicates the *Metrics* to his "beloved son
and colevite Cuthbert" for his instruction, "that as I have labored
to educate you in divine letters and ecclesiastical statutes, so also I
might instruct you in the metrical art, which is not unknown in
the divine books." He adds that he is subjoining a little book to
assist him; it is catalogued thus in the *History:* "And to this [*On
Metrics*] is added another small book on figures of speech or tropes,
that is, concerning the figures and modes of speech with which the
holy Scriptures are adorned" (*HE* V. 24, pp. 570–71). As an ex-
pansion of Donatus's *De schematibus* and *De tropis* (the last two sections
of the *Ars grammatica*), Bede clearly thought of the book with its
companion piece as a grammatical work; but editors and critics have
frequently, and even recently, called it a rhetorical treatise. This

confusion arises from the fact that vocational grammarians at an early date arrogated such topics to grammar from rhetoric, because figures of speech obviously applied to the study of language and its literary interpretation. The goals of the two disciplines, while sharing some identical topics, were distinct. Isidore in the *Etymologiae* was therefore compelled to include the treatment of figural speech twice, once under grammar in book I and again under rhetoric in book II. This wholesale inclusion of rhetorical matters within the pale of grammar allowed monastic grammarians like Bede to avoid espousing suspect rhetoric in the abbey school, while permitting a study of metrics and literary devices for interpretation of poetry in the Bible and Christian authors.[26] As a sort of appendix to grammar, treatises on figures were often treated as separate entities and circulated independently of other grammatical texts.[27]

One remarkable aspect of Bede's manual is that it is the first to give not a single example from Roman pagan literature, not even Virgil, whom he included in the *De arte metrica*. Only three examples are not scriptural, and those are from Christian poets. Earlier authors, such as Isidore in the *Etymologies,* Cassiodorus in his *Expositio Psalmorum,* and Julian of Toledo in *De vitiis et figuris,* had included scriptural references in their treatises, but Bede is the first to totally exclude pagan examples. The effect of this bold approach of dispensing with the classics is to assert the priority and preeminence of the biblical text. Bede thereby puts into pedagogical practice Augustine's theory in *De doctrina christiana,* books 3 and 4, that Scripture should serve as the basic text for the education of the Christian.[28] As Bede states in the prologue:

The Greeks pride themselves on having invented these figures or tropes. But, my beloved son, in order that you and all who wish to read this work may know that Holy Scripture surpasses all other writings not merely in authority because it is divine, or in usefulness because it leads to eternal life, but also for its age and artistic composition, I have chosen to demonstrate by means of examples collected from Holy Scripture that teachers of secular eloquence in any age have not been able to furnish us with any of these figures and tropes which did not appear first in Holy Scripture. (pp. 142–43)

A second remarkable feature of this treatise is that it is the first to attempt a synthesis of linguistic and theological symbolism in a grammatical treatise. Structured according to Donatus's system of

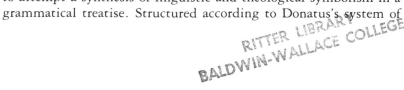

seventeen *schemata* (figures, the artistic ordering of words) and thirteen *tropi* (tropes, transferred meanings), Bede goes through each,
furnishing for each a definition and at least one example, usually
explained, until near the end. When he comes to allegory, he obviously felt that Donatus's treatment was inadequate to deal with
even the ordinary Christian hermeneutics common since the fourth
century. In the light of the exegetical techniques of the Fathers and
in view of Bede's own fondness for allegorical interpretation of
Scripture, it is easy to understand why Bede adds to this section on
allegory. Although Donatus had a brief section on the trope of
allegory, listing its seven species (Keil, *Grammatici latini* 4:401),
Bede first dilates the section by furnishing scriptural examples for
each of the seven types and then adds an important adjunct: the
division between factual and verbal allegory (pp. 164–66). He is
really attempting a general theory of symbol. The treatment is
grounded on Augustine's discussion of sign and symbol in book II
of *On Christian Doctrine* and his distinction made in the *De trinitate*
between *allegoria quae factis fit* (allegory in historical events, deeds)
and *allegoria quae verbis fit* (allegory in words, language). What is
unique in Bede is the attempt to yoke all of this under the rules of
grammar. To a modern philosophic linguist, his attempt is not
successful, since factual allegory depends on the objective realities
of history (e.g., Abraham's having two sons prefigures God's having
two peoples, Jewish and gentile), whereas verbal allegory, as Bede
teaches elsewhere, is metaphorical and ambiguous (e.g., an eagle
can symbolize Christ and much else; the moon can symbolize in-
constancy or the Church).[29] But Bede's synthesis of the various
symbolic modes established exegetical categories until Scholasti-
cism. Furthermore, Bede might have argued from Pauline, Augustinian, and Gregorian perception that even given the polyvalence
of verbal symbols, there exists a certain inherent propriety and
rightness within the sign itself to make it essentially analogous to
factual symbol. Factual and verbal allegory he applies to the traditional four modes of scriptural interpretation, classically formu-
lated by Cassian in book XIV of his *Conferences* and by Gregory in
the *Moralia:* literal (historical), typical, tropological (moral), and
anagogic (pp. 166–69).[30] As he so often does in his commentaries
and histories, Bede, in closing the section on allegory, calls upon
Gregory as his exemplar: "My discussion of the Church according
to the allegorical interpretation has followed the example of that

most learned exegete Gregory, who in his *Moralia* was accustomed to call allegory specifically those sayings and deeds which he interpreted figuratively concerning Christ or the Church" (p. 169).[31]

Unlike Bede's two systematic grammatical texts just discussed, which are structured according to topics, the little book *De orthographia* is organized on a totally different principle. He himself describes it as "a book about orthography, arranged according to the order of the alphabet" (*HE* V.24, pp. 570–71). Roughly alphabetized by first letter, after a quick run-through of single letter abbreviations (e.g., "L by itself stands for Lucius"), it consists entirely of short entries about the meaning and correct usage or spelling of words likely to cause difficulties for a medieval Latinist (e.g., *Caedo cecidi per .ae. diphthongon: "Caeditur et tilia ante iugo leuis"*— *Virgilius; cedo cessi per .e. simplicem* ("The verb *caedo, cecidi,* to cut, is spelled with an *ae* diphthong, as in this verse from Virgil's *Georgics;* but the verb *cedo, cessi,* to withdraw, has a simple *e*"). Compiled from seven grammatical works, the examples are drawn from both pagan and Christian texts, and the entries often give Greek equivalents to the Latin words, as found in the source texts. Until recently it has been assumed that Bede, who provides no preface or introduction, randomly and capriciously assembled the words and intended the collection to be used in the classroom. The classicist Anna Dionisotti, however, has astutely and convincingly argued from what Bede did with his sources and the nature of the resulting rearranged manual that Bede has produced a lexical key to grammatical, orthographic, and semantic information, something of a medieval counterpart to Fowler's *Modern English Usage;* Bede's manual is designed for the library, or scriptorium, or the desk of the scholarly monk.[32] So, whereas the other grammatical works were clearly intended as classbooks, this piece more likely served the function of a reference book for the educated reader or writer.

When did Bede assemble these grammatical tracts? He does not say. In the past scholars opined that they were all written early; however, their judgment was founded on shaky evidence. The *De arte metrica* and the *De schematibus et tropis* were ostensibly assigned an early date because Bede addresses Cuthbert as *conleuita,* usually understood as "fellow deacon," and therefore anterior to Bede's ordination to the next grade, the priesthood. In medieval Latin, however, *conleuita* can simply mean "fellow cleric."[33] The *De orthographia* was considered "even less mature" than the *De arte metrica* until Dionisotti pointed out that a correction Bede made in the *Retractatio* to his *Expositio* on Acts (6:8), concerning the meaning of the name Stephen, was already correctly interpreted in *De orthographia*, line 1082 (CCSL 123A, p. 50). That suggests that the *Expositio* (completed after 709) predated *De orthographia*. This runs counter to the general assumption that since the grammatical pieces are brief school works, they should antedate the more sophisticated scholarly works.

Tracts on Nature and Time

As part of the basic curriculum, Bede composed another little treatise, *De natura rerum*, which he called "a separate book on the nature of things" (*HE* V.24, pp. 570–71). It serves as an introduction to cosmology, a companion to the hexameron (exegesis on the first six days of creation in Genesis), and an adjunct to computus (measurement and time reckoning).[34] Reworking unsatisfactory tracts on nature, Isidore's *Liber rotarum* (also called *De natura rerum*) and pseudo-Isidore's *De ordine creaturarum*, Bede created a new text, incorporating much from about half of the Roman encyclopedist Pliny's *Natural History*, carefully edited and reordered. As was his frequent custom (rare in the Middle Ages) in his biblical commentaries, Bede credited the sources from which he drew his material with a marginal citation.[35] Although much of the book appears simpleminded and naive to readers in our scientific and technological age, his description of natural phenomena is as intelligent, organized, and rational as any to be found in the early Middle Ages. It is certainly a great improvement over Isidore's *De natura*.[36]

Bede opens the work with a prefatory poem of a couple distichs:

> Naturas rerum uarias labentis et aeui
> Perstrinxi titulis, tempora lata citis,
> Beda Dei famulus. Tu fixa obsecro perennem
> Qui legis astra, super mente tuere diem. (CCSL 123A, p. 189)

(I, Bede, servant of God, have summarized in brief notices the various natures of things and the broad periods of the passing age. You who read the stars, I beseech you, look with fixed mind above to the everlasting day.)

(A later gloss remarks about this little effort, "fuit enim Beda versificator tolerabilis" ["Bede was a tolerable versifier"], PL 90.188.)

In fifty-one brief chapters Bede explains the earth, the heavens with the stars, the planets with their orbits, and then the atmospheric events, the oceans and some rivers, the earth as a globe, cause of earthquakes and the volcanic activity of Aetna, and ends with the geographical divisions of the earth.

In the preface of the *De temporum ratione* (CCSL 123B, p. 263), Bede alludes to the *De natura* and the *De temporibus* as earlier works, but how early they are we do not know. In chapter 38 of the *De natura* he accepts Pliny's eight-year tidal cycle, which he corrects in chapter 29 of *De temporum ratione* to a nineteen-year cycle. The modern editor of *De natura* would place it even earlier than 703, the date of *De temporibus*.[37] It may indeed be that early, but that does not mean that Bede abandoned the subject entirely for other pursuits; on his deathbed he was again correcting material in Isidore's *Liber rotarum (De natura rerum)* for his students (Letter of Cuthbert in *HE,* p. 582).

Near the beginning (703) and near the end (725) of his distinguished writing career, Bede composed works on time and its calculation: "A separate book on chronology; also, a longer book on chronology" (*HE* V.24, pp. 570–71).[38] For the early Middle Ages the correct reckoning of time and dating of secular and sacred events was no easy matter. It is a subject of which Bede became the master. In the later Middle Ages treatises on chronology bore the name *computus* and Bede's tracts are called that, though in his day the word still meant the technique of counting and reckoning especially as applied to creating and understanding ecclesiastical calendars. The first computistical manual, *De temporibus liber,* is a revision and correction of books V and VI of Isidore's *Etymologies* and Irish supplements.[39] The book has twenty-two chapters, each only a brief paragraph in length. Chapters 1 through 16 treat of time from the shortest measures to the longest: minutes, hours, days, months, years (including solstice and equinox, seasons, Easter time reckoning), centuries, and finally the six ages of the world. Chapters 17–22 are a short chronicle giving the most important events in salvation history of each of the six ages, thus illustrating practically the preceding theory. (These chronicle chapters sometimes circulated as a separate work during the Middle Ages, as did the fuller chronicle at the end of *De temporum ratione.*)

As the frequency of the theme in his works confirms, Bede was extremely fond of the doctrine of the six ages of the world, which he inherited from Augustine and Isidore, and which clearly appealed to his orderly mind and strong sense of divine architectual planning. The six ages correspond to the six days of the creation in Genesis and the traditional six periods of human life from infancy to decrepitude (*De temporibus,* chap. 16, CCSL 123C, pp. 600–601; in *De temporum ratione,* chap. 66, CCSL 123B, p. 463, he makes the comparison yet more explicit by calling the human being a microcosm and a little world). Bede shared the common belief, therefore, that he was living in the last awful age before the final destruction. Where he differed was in the actual reckoning of the number of years in each age; instead of blindly accepting the figures that Isidore had unquestioningly taken from Jerome's translation of Eusebius's *Chronicle,* he himself calculated the time differences allotted in the Bible according to Jerome's translation from the Hebrew, with assistance from the historian Josephus where the Bible is unspecific. The result was that instead of the usual figure of more than 5000 years from the creation to the birth of Christ, Bede arrived at 3952 years. Such a disparity caused some eyebrow raising in Northumbrian clerical circles, with the result that five years after releasing *De temporibus* (708), Bede was accused of heresy at a banquet in the monastery of Hexham at which his diocesan superior Bishop Wilfrid was present. He was charged with positing Christ's birth in the fifth age instead of at the correct time, the beginning of the sixth. Bede, who ardently detested anything smacking of heresy and who also ardently considered time and God's work in time a serious matter, was appalled at this drunken attack by "wanton rustics." He responded to the report brought him by the Hexham monk and friend Plegwin with a ferocious letter (CCSL 123, pp. 617–26), demanding that the detailed justification it contained be read in the presence of the bishop before whom no one had defended him.

The youthful piece, *De temporibus,* also caused another problem. It was too condensed for students to absorb. Bede remedied this by producing a new version, called by Bede the *De temporibus liber maior* (*HE* V.24, pp. 570–71) but traditionally known as the *De temporum ratione.* It appeared some twenty-two years after the first. The reason for the delay can be surmised from the preface, which reveals Bede's continued rancorous concern over the earlier charge of heresy occasioned by the first book. Bede had not remained completely silent on computistical matters in the meantime; at some point he wrote a formal letter to Helmwald concerning solar increments; this he later incorporated into the *De temporum ratione* as chapters 38 and 39. In the preface, paraphrasing Jerome and naming with him Augustine, Eusebius, and Josephus as his precedents, Bede carefully serves notice that his decision to follow for his guide in this work the purity of the Hebraic Truth (that is, Jerome's Vulgate translation) is not intended as a slight to those chronographers who have followed the Septuagint (and its Old Latin) version of the Bible. He offers the work to his abbot Hwætberht for inspection and correction, and justifies his bringing still another computus to the world by quoting Augustine's words in the *De trinitate* (I.3, 25–28): "It is necessary for many books to be made by many, in diverse manner but not in diverse faith, even about the same questions, so that the subject itself may get through to many, in one way to some, in another to others." Then he ends, speaking for himself, saying that he has collected this material at the request of his brothers and if anyone takes offense or finds it superfluous, that person, maintaining fraternal charity, should go search the Fathers himself.

After an initial elementary chapter on finger calculation and a table of Greek and Roman letters signifying numbers, he has a chapter on the various aspects of time and historical modes of its measurement (e.g., Olympiads [Greek time reckoning by four year intervals between Olympian Games], indictions [fifteen-year cycle used as a Roman chronological unit], lunar and solar years). In chapter 3 and onwards he proceeds, as he did in *De temporibus* but in much greater detail and with much added material, from the smallest to the largest units of time. He discusses the day, week, and month. After his description of the Roman months and dating (chaps. 12–13) and the Greek months (chap. 14), he provides a chapter on English months, *De mensibus Anglorum,* with precious data for the students of Germanic and Anglo-Saxon culture. He does this, "for it seems to me incongruous to speak of the annual reckoning of other peoples and to be silent about my own people's" (p. 329). Since the English adopted the Roman calendar at an early date, Bede is really our only source for most of the information given here about the Anglo-Saxon months and the gods to whom they were dedicated. For instance, our only clue to the Anglo-Saxon deities Hretha and Eostre (Easter) is found here; there are valuable remarks about Giuli (Yule) and Blotmonath (Bloodmonth, the month of sacrifice), and other lore otherwise lost.[40] Bede then concludes this section with a chapter on the twelve signs of the zodiac.

Next, he treats all lunar movements, continuing on to the seasons and the solar movements. After analyzing the year, he concludes with a section, most important for him and his students, on the right reckoning of the Easter dates. The next to last chapter of this first part, chapter 66, beautifully presents the mystical or allegorical meaning of the Easter date, which he draws from Augustine's Letter 55, using his own lovely style. (Part of this chapter appears in the letter to King Nectan attributed to Ceolfrith in the *Ecclesiastical History* V.21, pp. 542–44, and makes us suspect that Bede at least composed the draft of the letter for Ceolfrith.) Bede climaxes the book with a consideration of the ages of the world. These chapters are termed the *chronica maiora* and like the *chronica minora* of *De temporibus* often circulated independently during the Middle Ages; this is especially true of chapter 66, on events of the sixth age. He greatly dilates the chronicle of the sixth age with over seventy pages of European events (to the year of the world 4680, the year 729, during which "the Saracens besieged Constantinople with an immense army"), includes chapters on the remainder of the sixth age, Augustine's ideas on the time of Christ's Second Coming, and the times of the Antichrist. The final chapter, 71, adds two more ages to the six of *De temporibus:* the seventh age is the unfinished age of all the souls of the blessed from the death of Abel to the Last Judgment; the eighth age is the age of eternal joy or eternal woe after the end of this world. On this serene note he concludes: "Therefore, my book about the rolling and tossing flow of the times, having also told of the eternal stability and stable eternity, may come to a suitable end" (p. 544).

A formal brief letter (CCSL 123C, pp. 635–42) to an otherwise unknown monk named Wicthed constitutes a sort of appendix to the *De temporum ratione;* it was often associated with that work in Bedan manuscript transmissions. The letter wrestles with the Anatolian Canon concerning the dating of Easter (cited by Bede in chapter 30 of *De temporum ratione*), which was not recognized as a forgery until the Renaissance. Running counter to orthodox reckoning, it was used by the Irish as an authority against the Roman dating for Easter. Not skirting the issue, Bede judges that the text at some point must have been corrupted, perhaps deliberately (sec. 11, p. 641).

Bede considered all these didactic treatises, grammatical and scientific, as propaedeutics to the study of Scripture. He neither disdained nor neglected these basics; for they extend from one end of his teaching career to the other, and from the simplicity of the early grammatical texts to the sophisticated, delicate complexity of the *De temporum ratione,* an immensely popular work throughout the Middle Ages. Moreover, he wrote these as tools for the schoolmaster, to serve him in viva voce teaching. As he remarks while discussing the signs of the zodiac in *De temporum ratione,* chapter 16, "Much more could be said here, but that is better done by a speaker than a writer."

Chapter Three
The Exegetical Works

Today Bede is known mainly as an historian; in his own time and throughout the Middle Ages he was known primarily as an exegete. Although his *Ecclesiastical History,* edited and translated many times, has been the subject of numerous studies and the author's qualities as an historian have been frequently examined, there is no comprehensive study of his exegesis or of his talents as an interpreter.[1] Nonetheless, the greatest portion of his writings are literary interpretations of biblical books. Actually, all his works relate to his exegetical profession and are affected by it. In his brief biographical note he says exactly that: "I have devoted myself entirely to the study of the Scriptures. . . . I have made it my business for my own benefit and for that of my brothers briefly to note and gather from the works of the venerable Fathers on the holy Scriptures, or to augment them in accordance with the manner of their meaning and interpretation" (*HE* V.24, p. 566). He then appends a nearly complete but nonchronological list of the works he had completed by the time he was fifty-nine, and he places first his treatises on biblical subjects, beginning with the Old Testament, Genesis, and ending with the Book of Revelation and summaries of readings on the whole of the New Testament (*HE* V.24, pp. 566–69). A few of his exegetical works have been lost, but most are extant.[2]

Bede's Hermeneutics

The books of the Bible he chose to interpret are of two types: those that were already favorites of the Fathers, such as the commentaries on Genesis and on Luke, and those that were largely ignored by earlier exegetes, such as the commentaries on Ezra and Nehemiah and on the New Testament Catholic Epistles. Both filled pedagogical needs; the former display Bede's talents as an adapter and synthesizer, and the latter testify to Bede's originality within the exegetical tradition. The former he undertook in order to sift and collate the best of the Fathers' comments and to digest and simplify the material for the slower, less sophisticated English; the latter, in order to provide a complete supplement to the Fathers for his students and readers. In a prefatory letter to Eusebius (the name given Hwætberht because it means love and zeal for piety)[3] before he begins the commentary on the Apocalypse, he states: "I have planned to take into account the inertia of our nation, namely the English, which not long since, in the time of Pope Gregory, received the seed of faith and has cherished it only lukewarmly so far as reading is concerned; so I have set about not only to elucidate the meaning, but also to compress the substance. For plain brevity is usually better fixed in the memory than prolix discussion" (PL 93.134AB).

As he explains in the preface of *In principium Genesis* to Bishop Acca of Hexham (to whom he dedicated most of his commentaries and for whom he had such warm regard), "many have said much about the first part of the book of Genesis; they have left to posterity monuments of their ingenuity." He cites Basil, Ambrose, and particularly Augustine. He comments that they were so prolific and expansive that only the relatively wealthy could possess all their commentaries, and they were also so profound that only the more educated could understand them, so that he at Acca's request has made an anthology of all of them, "as from the most beautiful fields of a widely blooming paradise, for the needs of the weak" (CCSL 118A, p. 1). In his letter to Bede, appended to the preface to the commentary on Luke, Acca tells of requesting a reluctant Bede to do the labor despite the fact that Ambrose had already written on Luke, because "there are certain sections in blessed Ambrose's exposition so eloquent and elevated that they can only be understood by the more learned, but not by the uneducated and the disinclined of the present age" (CCSL 120, p. 5). So Bede thought of his commentaries on these well-investigated books of the Bible as popular recensions for his age.

Works that he alone interpreted or for which only partial commentaries existed before his expositions obviously filled gaps in the hermeneutic program. Many of these remained unique commentaries throughout the Middle Ages. These treatises usually lack the explanatory prefaces found in the first type, but some, such as the *Expositio Actuum Apostolorum,* allude to the service he himself has performed, recognizing his interpretative contributions as God-given (CCSL 120, p. 7, l. 120) but humbly conditioned by such qualifiers as "according to the mode of my littleness" (CCSL 121, p. 4).

It is clear from the contents of the commentaries themselves that Bede has in both types, the patristic anthology and his own exposition, closely followed the hermeneutic procedures of the Fathers, particularly Augustine and Gregory.[4] In the commentaries on Luke and Mark he carefully included marginal citations to the four Fathers (AV—Augustine, AM—Ambrose, H—Jerome, G—Gregory) for his excerpts from them, "lest I be said to steal the sayings of my elders and to compose these as my own" (CCSL 120, p. 7, ll. 105–15). Nonetheless, it is also clear that in both the anthological and original types he has made his own contribution, deciding which authority to follow, which opinion to incorporate and which to exclude, what comments to add, and what sort of synthesis to form. This he feels compelled to do because according to the gospel parable (Matt. 25:14–30) the talent he received from the Lord has to be used and developed with interest (PL 93.134A). Furthermore, like Gregory, Bede has a moral and pragmatic bent that he likes to incorporate into some of the Fathers' more intellectual and theological reflections.

With the exceptions of the pieces on biblical geography, *De locis sanctis (On the Holy Places)* and *Nomina regionum atque locorum de Actibus Apostolorum (The Names of the Regions and Places from the Acts of the Apostles),* and two tracts arranged as responses to problems, *Aliquot quaestionum liber (A Book on Certain Questions)* and *In Regum librum XXX quaestiones (Thirty Questions on the Book of Kings),* Bede's method of commentary is the usual early medieval one of the phrase-by-phrase exegesis of a biblical book, from beginning to end. Related to the practice of the monastic *lectio divina* whereby the text is scrutinized and affectively meditated upon and personally applied to oneself, this procedure elucidates various potentialities contained within even apparently simple expressions. But the process atomizes and fragments the text, allowing its thematic totality to be lost. For a reader searching for a consistent and structured development, such glossing can prove exasperating and even stupefying. Even Bede, whose historical and hagiographic writings reveal his abilities to frame and order a text coherently, follows the conventions of this genre, especially in his early exegesis, such as the commentary on the Apocalypse, by simply doing verse-by-verse explanations in brief discrete sections, a procedure he calls *commaticum* (PL 93.203A); however, he does furnish some guideposts that relate sections and highlight major themes.

Bede's task was eased by the knowledge he gained in his wide reading and retentive absorption of earlier hermeneutics. Through them he learned various methods for approaching the sacred text. One of these was the allegorical interpretative mode; the other, related method was the typological and tropic mode set down in the Rules of Tyconius. Both resulted from Hellenistic pagan and patristic attitudes toward literature. The word crafted by poetic and divine inspiration was understood to have a literal surface meaning but also a deeper, hidden, and spiritual meaning.[5] The literal meaning serves as the husk, outercovering, and metaphorical sign of the profound truth it embodies. Gregory and Bede point out that the Lord taught in parables and that he himself explained figuratively the parable of the sower in order to teach us also to look beneath the surface (*In Lucam* III.8, 4–5, CCSL 120, p. 173, ll. 309–12). For the Christian as for the rabbinical Jew, the sacred Scriptures are full of meaning, and nothing in them can be devoid of significance. Bede says, "The entire series of sacred utterance is replete with mystical figures, not only in words and deeds but times and places" (*In Genesim* III.14, 15, CCSL 118A, p. 188, ll. 1610–14), including names (*nomen est omen*), numbers, and symbols. This is an assertion of faith that Bede frequently repeats in his hermeneutics, citing Paul's statement, "All things happened to them in figure, but they are written for our instruction" (I Cor. 10:11): " 'all things,' not only deeds or words which are contained in the sacred Scriptures but truly also the relationships of places, hours, and seasons, and also the circumstances in which they are done or spoken" (*De tabernaculo* I.5–9, CCSL 119A, p. 5).[6]

In Alexandria, the center for the allegorical interpretative schools of Greek literature, Philo Judaeus (d. A.D. 45) combined the Platonic and Stoic allegorical method of construing literature (particularly Homer) with the rabbinical system of biblical commentary. The resultant procedure was used by the Christian patriarchs Clement and Origen, who also incorporated the Pauline teaching that the Old Testament prefigures or foreshadows the New. Their methodology was carried on in the West by Ambrose, Augustine, and Gregory. The Bible contains truth in all its divine complexity and interrelated aspects. In it the Christian exegete sees a "beautiful

sacramental concord" whereby nature and history serve as indicators
of higher truths (*In Lucam* II. 6, 1, CCSL 120, p. 127, l. 1088).
In the hands of a gifted literary exegete the allegorical method can
elicit from the biblical text profound meaning and poetic richness.
It can extricate the inner meanings of a pregnant phrase or complex
allusion. It can produce literary hermeneutic criticism. On the other
hand, it can also be a flight from the reality of the text to the
arbitrary and capricious world of intellectual fancy. It can divest
the text of cogency, immediate personal application, and power. It
can also lead to the absurd.

The alternative technique of literal, historical interpretation characteristic of the Antiochene school of commentators, Theodore of
Mopsuestia and John Chrysostom, was also transmitted in the West
by the *Instituta regularia divina* by Junilius.[7] In the early exegesis
of the British Isles, this method captivated the Irish (whose quaint
curiosity about every detail and the reason for it favored a concen-
tration on the historical) and it was also favored in the school of
Canterbury under Eastern-trained Theodore and Hadrian. Although
Bede was indebted to the Irish for much learning and admired the
teachers at the school of Canterbury, for his biblical exegesis he
returned to the tradition of the older Latin exegesis.[8] He is solidly
in the camp of the Western Fathers. Bede relies on Augustine for
doctrine and much of his exposition, but in interpretative spirit he
favors Gregory, with whom he shares a kind of spiritual affinity in
his monastic humility, magnanimous compassion, and pragmatic
realism.[9] He also shares Gregory's range of scriptural analysis from
hard historicity on one end of the spectrum to fantastic allegorical
flights found in the *Moralia in Job* on the other.

Bede found the treasures of God's message to be infinitely rich
and inexhaustible. In order to delve for them, Bede, like Augustine,
uses whatever exegetical tools and methods seem appropriate to the
immediate task. Therefore his exegetical practice is eclectic and
literary. Nevertheless, though his general procedure is allegorical
and sometimes exuberantly so, it is not exclusively so, since in such
works as his commentary on the Acts of Apostles and the *Retractatio*
he demonstrates an essentially historical approach. Bede follows
Augustine's mandates, set out in *On Christian Doctrine,* for adherence
to historical truth and orthodoxy. We are to trust the text at the
literal level first, provided it does not contradict the principle of
charity (III. 10 and 14). Even more than Gregory, Bede maintains

that the literal, historical meaning of the text must not be abandoned or surrendered entirely to the allegorical interpretation: "Whoever expends effort on the allegorical sense should not leave the plain truth of history in allegorizing (*In Genesim* I.1, CCSL 118A, p. 3, ll. 30–31; cf. *In Lucam* III.10, 29, CCSL 120, p. 222, ll. 2206–9). Although he shares the common rabbinical and Christian notion that the Song of Songs should not be understood in a carnal and literal sense, "but the whole thing wants to be understood spiritually and typically" (V.8, 1, CCSL 119B, p. 337, ll. 1–4), he sometimes excludes an allegorical interpretation in favor of a wholly literal one (*In I Samuhelem* II.15, 11, CCSL 119, p. 130, ll. 2625–30; also 15, 35, p. 136, ll. 2869–70). This he does when the literal meaning has immediate application to virtuous behavior for the reader. Given the saving norm of final reliance on the historical meaning, Bede's usual method of exposition, like other exegetes, is largely typological. He defends the allegorical stretching and even wrenching of the text by an appeal to the metaphor of crushing aromatic herbs in order to release their fragrance (*Homelia* 8, CCSL 122, p. 233, 4–8). He works now in one system of allegorical interpretation, now in another, guided by the rule of faith, traditional orthodoxy, and Christian charity.[10]

Quite often Bede simply presents a twofold relationship in a text, with a single allegorical interpretation superimposed upon the literal meaning. At other times he spreads out a threefold meaning, either historical, allegorical, and moral (e.g., *De tabernaculo* II, CCSL 119A, p. 91, ll. 1957–60) or historical, allegorical, and anagogic (e.g., *In I Samuhelem* II.10, CCSL 119, p. 87, ll. 799–824). Or, indeed, it can be the fourfold method of historical, typical or allegorical, tropological or moral, and anagogic. Bede was the definitive authority in the Middle Ages for this formulation.[11] The four feet on the tabernacle in *De tabernaculo* (CCSL 119A, p. 25) serve as an analogy for this way of interpreting Scripture. These four senses Bede again proposes in his beautiful commentary on the Song of Songs. Discussing the verse, "Your lips, my spouse, are dripping honeycomb" (4:11), he explains:

Honey in the wax is meaning of the divine utterances in the letter, which is rightly called dripping honeycomb: for the honeycomb drips when it has more honey than the wax containers can hold, because such is the fecundity of the holy Scriptures that a verse which is usually written within a brief line could fill many pages, if it were examined by scrutinizing the expressions more diligently for the great sweetness they more interiorly contain. Let us give one example. The Psalmist says, "Praise, O Jerusalem, the Lord" (147.1 [RSV 12]), because, according to the letter, as a citizen of that city, in which the temple of God was, he exhorts it to speak praises. But according to allegory Jerusalem is the Church of Christ spread over the whole earth; likewise, according to tropology, that is the moral sense, each soul is rightly called a holy Jerusalem; likewise, according to anagogy, that is the intelligence leading to things above, Jerusalem is the habitation of the celestial fatherland, which is made up of holy angels and men. (*In Cantica Canticorum* IV.11, CCSL 119B, p. 260)

These four scriptural senses described with the example of the fourfold meaning of Jerusalem Bede takes from a well-known passage in Cassian's *Conferences* (XIV.8, CSEL 13, p. 405). Bede goes on to show how the meanings though interconnected are yet distinct. In other words, he indicates that the terms of the analogy are not totally coextensive. He then returns to explain that the honeycomb is dripping "since the doctors of the Church either in legal prefiguration or in prophetic sayings or in the words of the Lord or in mystical events demonstrate the multiplex fullness of interior sweetness inherent in the text."

In the long passage from the *De tropis,* cited in the last chapter, Bede combines the doctrine of two types of allegory (deed and word) with that of the fourfold meaning.[12] "The allegory of word or of work figuratively signifies sometimes an historic thing, sometimes a typical, sometimes a tropological (that is, moral) lesson, sometimes anagogy (that is, a sense leading to things above)" (CCSL 123A, pp. 164–69). Since each of the four levels of meaning can be either of deed or of word or of both, the resulting combinations are so numerous that a single passage in Scripture would demand, Bede surmises, many pages for even a cursory exposition. Despite the brief stock examples he cites and the large potential for allegorical development he recognizes, in practice Bede never really analyzes the biblical text at hand according to the fourfold method. It is usually two- or at most threefold. In this he follows Gregory's practice. Furthermore, Bede uses various allegorical terms rather loosely and to some extent interchangeably: *figura, typus, mysterium, sacramentum, sensus (intelligentia) spiritalis* (figure, type, mystery, sacrament, spiritual sense, spiritual intelligibility).[13] Like Augustine, Bede is more concerned with elucidating the text in a literary critical way than in conforming to a rigid mode of doctrinaire theory; like Gregory, he is more eager to extract moral meaning than to pursue theological speculation.

Bede speaks of the "rules" and "laws" of allegory (e.g., *In Lucam* III.7, 37, CCSL 120, p. 167, l. 41). To some extent they apply to observing accepted meanings for some traditional biblical symbols, such as a dove for the Spirit: "Because the Holy Spirit descended upon the Lord (Luke 3:22), the word 'dove' or 'doves' rightly signifies the spiritual sense and gifts" (*In Cantica* I.1, 14, CCSL 119B, p. 208, ll. 686–89).[14] In a larger sense, though, by the rule of allegory Bede means the propriety and fitness of an analogy or figure as it conforms to the rule of faith and love. He is explicit about the norm of orthodoxy in *Quaestio* V of *Octo quaestionum liber,* where in setting straight the meaning of Romans 14:5, "Let every man abound in his own sense," he states, "If we are unable to arrive at the more sublime secrets of the divine mysteries, yet we may humbly and devoutly serve the Lord in those which we understand and perceive are truly to be believed and trusted"; for the rest, we are to follow the teaching of the great doctors in order to arrive at the high truths (PL 93.458AB). In *Quaestio* VI he tackles the problem of seemingly subjective interpretation of biblical texts, so that sometimes bad people and bad actions are held up as models and exemplary types. For instance, the liturgy of Holy Saturday associates the wicked Saul with the innocent Christ. "It ought not seem absurd to you that the evil acts of the reprobate should signify something good, or again that the good works of the just should bear a contrary signification." That is very common in Scripture (e.g., *In Genesim* IV, CCSL 118A, p. 236, ll. 1515–20) and in the Fathers (*In I Samuhelem* II, CCSL 119, pp. 91–92, ll. 993–1049), particularly Gregory (see *In Moralia* III.28, 55, PL 75.625C). Even though the good are truly just models, particular qualities or circumstances of the bad might allow a suitable meaning for good to be elicited, and vice versa. In other words, appealing to biblical and patristic precedents, Bede presents subjective, impressionistic, and even apparently foolish allegorical types and analogies for an ad hoc exegesis.[15]

In common with many ancient writers, the Fathers, and medieval exegetes generally, Bede shares a fondness for numerical symbolism, in accord with the great numerical expositor in Augustine's favored text, "You have ordered all things in measure, and in number, and in weight" (Wis. 11:21).[16]

By way of Augustine Bede learned a more specific set of exegetical techniques, the Rules of Tyconius.[17] Augustine had given the Donatist heretic Tyconius his due by extolling his seven rules as keys to expounding obscurities and subtextual assumptions in Scripture. These rules are really literary critical in that they involve exploitation of grammatical figures, where the Scripture says one thing so that another is understood. The rules try to list the various ambiguous or confusing predications that are made as the result of synecdoche or a similarly submerged figure. In the Letter to Eusebius (that is, Hwætberht) prefacing the *Expositio Apocalypseos Sancti Iohannis* (PL 93.129–34), Bede first states that the Apocalypse is structured in seven parts; he then keeps the symmetry of the heptad by outlining the seven Tyconian rules. The first concerns references to the Lord and his body: the mystical body (the Church) is distinct from the head but identified with it. The second is the twofold nature of the Church, made up of saints and sinners in the communion of faith and therefore both sinful and saintly, so that, for instance, she can be referred to as dark but lovely (Song of Songs 1:4). The third concerns the distinction of promises and the law, or the spirit and the letter, or grace and commandment. The fourth is about genus and species, or whole and parts. The fifth is about times and numbers and the various symbolic uses of them. The sixth is recapitulation, by which Bede, following Augustine, understands an anachronistic or dislocated time reference, by which one event is mentioned before its true chronological place. (For Tyconius, recapitulation meant the simultaneous speaking of the type and antitype, the promise and the fulfillment.) The seventh, about the devil and his body, is the completion and obverse of the first: as the Church is the body of Christ, so the wicked and particularly heretics are the body of the devil.

These rules Bede found useful in explicating the complex imagistic text of Revelation, and to some extent in his other commentaries, such as on Genesis, on the Tabernacle, and on the first book of Samuel.[18] For instance, he implicitly invokes rule one when in discussing David as a figure of Christ in book IV of *In I Samuhelem,* he points out that in certain actions, such as warfare against the Philistines, David represents individual Christians (CCSL 119, pp. 213–14, ll. 64–103). As in the *De schematibus et tropis,* we see Bede using analyses from his grammatical discipline in the service of exegesis.

In general, Bede's early exegetical treatises betray a much greater dependence on large patristic borrowings, whole sections being lifted from a source with some linking prose and occasional abbreviation. His later treatises, though still heavily indebted to the Fathers, as Bede candidly admits and proclaims, are more original, synthesizing traditional doctrine and personal observation, in which the sources are more expertly subsumed into the texture of the commentary. We could follow Bede's maturation as an exegete more specifically if we knew when each of his works was composed. Unfortunately, very few are definitely datable, and some of the pieces were composed in stages or are amalgams of earlier and later work. In a half dozen years, from about 725 to 731, Bede composed exegetical works with extraordinary energy and output. At least ten of his major commentaries were completed during that short period, while he was also working on the *Historia ecclesiastica*.[19] We can well understand why, as Cuthbert reports of his last days, he was still dictating in some haste on his deathbed.

Since we do not know exactly when they were written, the commentaries will not be discussed according to their date of composition but according to the order that Bede himself follows in his bibliography (*HE* V.24, pp. 566–69), the traditional order of the books in the Bible.

Commentaries on the Old Testament

"The beginning of Genesis up to the birth of Isaac and the casting out of Ishmael: four books" (*HE* V.24, pp. 566–67). Book I of Bede's *Commentary on Genesis,* as its introductory letter to Acca shows, belongs to the popular exegetical tradition of hexaëmera, that is, commentaries on the first six days of creation, some of which end with chapter 2:3, but others, like Bede's, end with 3:24, Adam's ejection from the Garden of Eden.[20] Book I is made up of two parts: Ia (Creation), related to Bede's works on time and nature, treats the physical world, chronology, and paschal calculation; it garners patristic hexaëmeral material in support of Bede's position, defended in the Letter to Plegwin, concerning the dating of the six ages in relationship to the six days of creation; Ib (the Fall) is a hasty assemblage of material extracted largely from Augustine's *De Genesi ad litteram*. By contrast, books II through IV reveal Bede's expertise in their authoritative treatment and careful structure, each ending

at a climactic point of salvation history. It is conjectured that Ia
was written about the time of his *Commentary on the Apocalypse*,
between 703–9, Ib around 725, and books II–IV after *In Esdram*
but before 731.

"The tabernacle, its vessels, and the priestly vestments: three
books." *De tabernaculo et uasis eius ac uestibus sacerdotum libri III* was
probably begun after *Genesis* was finished, sometime around 721.[21]
Bede announces in the first chapter (CCSL 119A, p. 5, ll. 1–9)
that he will speak about the figure of the tabernacle and its vessels
and utensils, prescribed in Exodus 24:12 to 30:21; he then proceeds
to discuss the reception of the tablets of the Law and those sacred
items of the tabernacle, according to their allegorical significations.
For instance, the variety of vessels indicates the variety of divine
utterances according to the unequal capacities of the hearers (I.830–
50); the base of the candelabra represents the Lord whose grace
branches out to his disciples (1145 ff.).

"The First Book of Samuel, to the death of Saul: four books."
Just as objects such as the tabernacle and the temple afforded Bede
opportunity for a strongly allegorical commentary, so in an analogous way some historical parts of the Bible were subjected to a
thorough allegorization. This is particularly true of *In primam partem
Samuhelis libri IIII.* Bede explains in his prologue to Acca that Samuel
is as prophetic as Jeremiah and Isaiah, but the circumstances of his
life have to be understood by the Christian, especially the cleric, in
a figural, nonliteral manner. For instance, the text states that Samuel's father Helcana had two wives; that is obviously not an appropriate model for the clergy. How will we be able to profit spiritually
"if from these and similar words we do not know how to carve out
an allegorical sense, which refreshes us interiorly in a lively way by
castigating, educating, and consoling?" (CCSL 119, p. 9, ll. 29–
34). We see therefore in the first reading of book I that the husband
is Christ, whose two wives represent by typology the synagogue
and the church (p. 11). The readings continue in a resolutely allegorical manner throughout, right to the last verse of the book
"and they fasted seven days" (1 Sam. 31:12), which gives Bede the
felicitous opportunity to bring in once again an analysis of the seven
ages (six of the world and the seventh of rest), the sixth hour when
Christ dies with the seventh of his repose, the seven days of carnal
observation and blindness until the eighth day of the Lord and his
resurrection (p. 272).

Many of Bede's greatest modern admirers have found the allegory in this work excessive.[22] That indicates a basic difference of religious literary taste, not an objective criticism of the work. What Bede is doing here he does very well, adroitly, and even daringly. It seems possible that *In I Samuhelem* could again have admirers, especially among literary symbolic interpreters, as it did in the eighth century, when Bishop Lul implored Archbishop Æthelberht of York to send him a copy of it (*EHD* I, no. 188, pp. 834–35).

"On the building of the temple, an allegorical interpretation like the others: two books." *De templo* was composed towards the end of Bede's career: he mentions it in his letter to Acca, accompanying a copy of the *Historia ecclesiastica,* in which he speaks of the *De templo* as having been recently finished and sent.[23] In the prologue Bede explains that he has "written in the allegorical mode about the building of the temple of God, following the pathways of the great treatises" (CCSL 119A, p. 144, ll. 55–59). After equating the Temple of Solomon by figure with the universal Church, Bede examines the structure of the temple, described in 3 Kings:5–7 (RSV 1 Kings), and 2 Paralipomenon:2–5 (RSV 2 Chronicles), often both on a literal and allegorical level. That is, he sorts out the materials, directions, arrangements, and measurements of the parts of the temple as a prior literal basis for his more extensive allegorical interpretation.

"On the book of Kings: thirty questions." *In Regum librum XXX* [*triginta*] *quaestiones* is, according to the prologue to Nothelm, a response to inquiries about the meaning of thirty puzzling passages in the four books of Kings. He says he will answer the questions by "following the paths of the Fathers" (CCSL 119, p. 293, line 23), but that apparently means according to their spirit because other than a half dozen borrowings from Josephus and Jerome, the answers, all relatively brief, are his own. Many are literal and textual, dealing with such matters as variant readings (III, p. 298, "what your codex has is entirely false"), the use of hyperbole (VIII, p. 302), or a puzzling detail (such as X, p. 303, why snowy days enable Banaia to slay a lion in a pit). Some are allegorical, however, such as Samuel prefiguring Christ (I, p. 296).

"On the Proverbs of Solomon: three books." Bede begins the *In Proverbia Salomonis libri III* with a gloss on the word "parables" of Proverbs 1:1 (Vulgate), stating that "Solomon gave the book this name so that we know to understand the higher meaning and not the literal in what he says" in the same way Christ intended us to understand his parables (CCSL 119B, p. 23, ll. 1–7). A portion of the commentary is allegorical, and the last section on chapter 31:10–31 (pp. 149 ff.) is completely spiritualized by identifying the "strong woman" with Holy Church. Much of the central commentary is, however, simply a didactic, practical explication of the maxims. In this treatise we can learn much of Bede's own wisdom, his attitudes about educational theory, Christian behavior and virtue, and societal norms. For instance, commenting on the passage "For I was a tender young son of my father and only child of my mother" (4:3), he says, "Nothing encourages the mind in the hope of acquiring wisdom more than when we recall that those whom we now admire as shining in wisdom were once little children and unlearned" (p. 45). [24] On the passage "The hearing ear and the seeing eye, the Lord has made them both" (20:12), he remarks in part, "No one should despise the simplicity of a brother, who even though less learned for preaching is ready to learn or to accomplish the good things which he has learned; but he should recall that he who gave him the grace of greater knowledge, has granted spiritual gifts to that brother; nor has he given the gifts he wanted to for the benefit of him alone but also for the welfare of the brother, giving to each as he does according to the measure of his donation" (p. 105). On 24:5 he reminds us that the wise man need not be strong physically (p. 121). Bede's commentary is based in part on an allegorical commentary on Proverbs by the fifth-century bishop Salonius;[25] but on a larger scale, his exegesis represents a continuation of age-old pagan and Judeo-Christian sapiential literature.

"On the Song of Songs, seven books." The first book, which in CCSL 119B is treated as a preface (pp. 167–80), constitutes, as Bede explains at the beginning (p. 167) and again in the last book (p. 359), a refutation against the fifth-century Pelagian polemicist and sharp-witted enemy of Augustine, Julian of Eclanum; "the volume is in defense of the grace of God which he impugned." After assigning each section of the Song to one of three speakers, Synagogue, Church, and Christ (pp. 185–89), Bede follows with five books of commentary, in which under the figure of the spouse and his beloved is understood Christ and his Church or, tropologically, every Christian soul (I, p. 190, ll. 1–7). The lovely commentary, so much in the spiritualistic mode traditional since Origen, contains nonetheless a wealth of naturalistic lore. For instance, he describes the qualities of cedar and cyprus (pp. 209–10, ll. 763–77, pp. 264–65, ll. 797–809) and gives a lengthy disquisition on the nature of the mandragora (pp. 335–36). The last book is made up of various extracts from Gregory pertaining to the Song, here collected, "reckoning that it would be more pleasant for readers, if that which he scattered throughout all his works, were collected together in a single book" (p. 359, ll. 10–15).

"On Ezra and Nehemiah: three books." When Bede wrote his preface to Genesis (probably between 703 and 709), he stated that he intended to look into the book of Esdras, but in the commentary itself (CCSL 119A, pp. 343–44, ll. 155–57) he refers to a passage in the *De temporum ratione,* which places the completed *In Ezram et Neemiam* chronologically after 725. In the prologue to Acca, he outlines his purpose in commenting on the books of Ezra and Nehemiah (Vulgate 1 and 2 Esdras): "to discover, with the outer cortex being stripped away, the other higher, more sacred substance in the pith of the spiritual sense, which indeed signifies by prophetic figures but clear intention the Lord himself and his temple and his city (which we are)" (p. 237, ll. 12–17). He follows his usual allegorical procedure of laying the foundation by explaining the literal meaning and circumstances if they are not evident before building the spiritual superstructure. Thus, for 1 Esdras 3:1 (I, p. 263, ll. 878 ff.) he points out that the seventh Hebrew month is our October, especially honored because it was the month during which the temple was dedicated. Then he talks about the higher sense, in which "the seventh month indicates the grace of the Holy Spirit which in Isaiah the prophet and in the Apocalypse of St. John is described as septiform," and then, in a moral sense, how we are "Israel as one man gathered in Jerusalem."

"On the Song of Habakkuk, one book." Bede tells us that "a beloved sister in Christ" (that is, a nun) requested this short commentary on the magnificent third chapter of Habakkuk. "The hymn proclaims especially the mysteries of the Lord's passion," for which reason it is used in the office for sext of Holy Saturday and in lauds each Friday. But for Bede it contains much else. "It also describes mystically the event of the incarnation, resurrection, and ascension into the heavens, as well as of the faith of the nations and the perfidy of the Jews." Moreover, in its lamentation for the innocent and complaint about the guilty it is as if the prophet viewed the deplorable state of the present era (CCSL 119B, p. 381).

"On the book of the blessed father Tobias, an allegorical explanation concerning Christ and the Church: one book." This commentary on Tobit, another first in Christian tradition, is also a brief but rich allegoresis. "The book of holy father Tobias opens to its readers much that is wholesome at the literal level as one might expect from a work that abounds in great examples and admonitions of moral life; and if one who knows how to interpret it historically also goes at it allegorically, he sees that it stands out in inner meaning against its literal simplicity like an apple among leaves" (CCSL 119B, p. 3, ll. 1–7). In commenting on Tobit's blinding by the swallow's excrement, Bede once again reminds us that "allegorically sometimes good signifies bad, and sometimes good things signify the bad deeds of men; for if that were not permitted, 'God is light' would never be written with black ink but always with shining gold, and indeed although you could write the name of the devil in white chalk it still signifies profound darkness" (p. 5, ll. 1–8).

Commentaries on the New Testament

"On the Gospel of Mark: four books." Composed some years after his commentary on Luke, as he says in the prologue (CCSL 120, p. 432, ll. 48–50), the commentary on Mark includes large blocks of the Lucan commentary frequently when the two synoptics have concurrent texts. Nonetheless, this commentary manifests some of Bede's finest and most mature exegesis. Although he often and with due credit interweaves appropriate sections from the Fathers, his own contribution is intelligent and extensive. In the first section (pp. 437–38), for instance, he discusses on his own the interesting fact that the Gospels all have different time frames, and the appropriateness of those differences. Although in this work he mostly explicates the texts on a literal and historical level, he does not hesitate to indicate a tropological meaning when suitable. Thus, commenting on Mark 11:11, "And he entered Jerusalem, and went into the temple," he edifyingly remarks: "The fact that having entered the city he first visited the temple presages for us a form of piety which we follow. When we enter a village or town or some other locale in which there is a house of prayer consecrated to God, we should first turn aside to that, and after we have commended ourselves to the Lord through the pursuit of prayer, we can then leave to do those temporal affairs for which we have come" (p. 575, ll. 1296–1303).

He also eagerly calls attention to important spiritual meanings on the allegorical level that the text suggests. For instance, in the subsequent passage, which describes Christ's driving the money changers from the temple, after noting how the church can also be polluted by gossip and chatter, he points out that the individual soul is the temple that the Lord cleanses and purifies (ll. 1415–75).

"On the Gospel of Luke: six books." The prologue begins with a letter of Bishop Acca pleading with Bede to do the arduous task of a commentary on this Gospel even though it has been commented on by Ambrose and others but in too erudite a fashion for English students. Bede responds by pointing out how he has gone about the difficult task and explaining his careful use and citation of patristic sources (CCSL 120, p. 7, ll. 109–11). He then notes that "some things which the Lord of light has revealed I have added as marks of my own sweat, when it seemed opportune." He hastens to point out, though, that those who have accused him of idiosyncratic originality, as, for instance, in his assigning the symbol of the lion to Matthew and of the man to Mark in his earlier commentary on the Apocalypse, ought to realize that it was not his notion but Augustine's.[26] He then quotes Augustine at length from the *De consensu evangelistarum* to prove it.

A good example of Bede's original contribution to biblical exegesis comes in his commentary on Luke 23:34, "But Jesus said, 'Father, forgive them for they know not what they do.' " Bede recognized a historical and exegetical problem: if Jesus asked forgiveness for his killers, how was it that God sanctioned the punishment of the Jews by the destruction of Jerusalem and its temple? Therefore, turning from Ambrose's and Augustine's opinion that the Jews were blindly ignorant of Christ's divinity, Bede makes the following distinction: "It should be noted indeed that he offered prayers to the Father not for those who, fired by malice and pride, preferred to crucify the one they understood to be the Son of God rather than acknowledge him, but instead for those specifically who, possessing the zeal of God but not according to wisdom, did not realize what they were doing" (CCSL 120, pp. 402–3, ll. 1583–93).[27]

"On the Acts of the Apostles: two books." One of the books is the *Actuum Apostolorum expositio,* written in some haste (CCSL 121,

p. 3, l. 15) soon after 709 and dedicated to Acca. The other, called a retraction in conscious imitation of Augustine's reassessment of his works, is a book containing corrections, reconsiderations, and revisions of the first version; it was probably written sometime between 725 and 731, and it demonstrates not only Bede's surer hand as an exegete but also his much firmer grasp on the Greek language.[28] "Now I am inserting into that volume a brief little book of retraction, expressly for the purpose of adding to what was said too meagerly and correcting what seemed otherwise than apt. Also in it I have tried to note briefly certain expressions which I have seen put more or less otherwise in the Greek" (p. 103).

Working with at least three Latin and two Greek versions of Acts, Bede manifests great sensitivity to textual variants and to critical readings. He brings all his learning—grammatical, literary, exegetical—to the careful reading and interpretation of Luke's text. Here is just one small example of his meticulousness: "I wrote in the preceding book that Stephen meant 'crowned'; and what I wrote was not far from the truth. However, learning more precisely, I discovered that in Greek Stephen does not mean 'crowned' but 'crown,' and this name is of the masculine gender and therefore quite suitable for a man among them." (VI.8, p. 130, ll. 14–19).

Both Bede's studies of Acts demonstrate not only his exegetical skills but also his historical interests and investigative penchant. In his commentaries on Acts 2:42–47 and 4:32–37 (pp. 23, 27, 118, and especially 126–27), Bede accepted the traditional ahistoric reading of these passages about the primitive Christian church as a model monastic community, distinguished by the abandonment of worldly goods and the practice of perfect love. As Glenn Olsen has pointed out, however, "there was in Bede's mind a second, more historically minded, tendency to see the primitive Church as having passed through stages of development. . . . He was able to see that Christianity itself had passed through stages of development, beginning with a period in which Jewish influences were pronounced and passing into a period in which the distinctiveness of Christian teaching became more apparent. A close reading of the Acts of the Apostles suggested to him that not all the first Christians abandoned private property and took up celibacy."[29]

"On the Apostle [Paul], I have transcribed in order whatever I found in the works of St. Augustine." This *collectaneum* on the Pauline Epistles, which exists in only seven manuscripts, has never been printed.[30] It demonstrates that Bede, like Peter of Tripoli (before 550) and Florus of Lyons afterwards (ninth century), recognized the close theological link between Paul and Augustine, and thought it worthwhile to anthologize passages by the latter on the former.

"On the seven Catholic Epistles: one book each." The seven short letters placed before the Apocalypse at the end of the New Testament—James; 1 and 2 Peter; 1, 2, and 3 John; and Jude—received little attention by exegetes before and even after Bede. Augustine had fashioned a commentary on 1 John, which Bede used in his commentary on that letter, but for the rest he was on his own, commandeering an occasional pertinent text or patristic animadversion.[31] Although this treatise is one of Bede's earlier works, it was apparently the most popular of all his commentaries.[32] Like most of his other early exegesis, excluding the commentary on Revelation, this commentary is mostly literal and historical and lacks the long allegorical flights characterizing the late exuberance of *De tabernaculo* and *In 1 Samuhelem.* It has Bede's usual strong bent for moral application. For instance, just after speaking about the justifying works of Abraham, James asks, "Was not the harlot Rahab made righteous from works?" (2:25), to which Bede remarks:

Lest they plead that they are not strong enough to imitate the works of such a great ancestor as Abraham, especially since no one now would compel them to offer their sons to God to be killed but God himself through the Scriptures prohibited this, he adds also the example of a woman, an iniquitous woman, a foreign woman. Yet she, by works of mercy, by showing hospitality to the servants of God even at risk to her life, deserved to be made righteous from sins, to be enrolled as a member of the people of Israel, to be counted on the list of their royal lineage, to mingle with the families of our Lord and savior himself [cf. Matt. 1:5]. (CCSL 121, p. 205, ll. 284–93, trans. D. Hurst, pp. 33–34)

"On the Apocalypse of St. John: three books." Composed between 703 and 709, *In Apocalypsin* is also very early (maybe the earliest of all) and was also very popular. Unlike the commentary on the seven Epistles, however, it is strongly allegorical, an approach that the text itself with its use of symbolism and mystery mandates. It displays an extraordinary dependence on the comments of the Fathers and earlier exegetes. Its entries are brief and abrupt, as is typical of the *commaticum* format. For example, " 'And I saw in the right

hand of him who was seated on the throne a book written inside
and outside' (5:1). This vision demonstrates the mysteries of sacred
Scripture laid open by the incarnation of the Lord. Its concordant
unity contains the Old Testament as outside and the New as inside"
(PL 93.145A). However, when he comes to explain the significance
of the twelve precious stones that form the foundations of the heavenly Jerusalem (Rev. 21:19–20), Bede draws extensively upon numerous sources of lapidary lore (Pliny, Solinus, Epiphanius, Jerome,
Ambrose, Gregory, Isidore, Anglo-Latin glosses and the Hiberno-
Latin tract *De duodecim lapidibus,* and possibly the Latin Damigeron)
to present an original systematic exposition of the text. He concludes
the extended passage with this comment: "I may perhaps seem to
have set forth these remarks concerning the precious stones at greater
length than belonged to the *commaticum* mode of interpretation. For
it was necessary diligently to expound their natures and provenance,
then very carefully to investigate their sacred meaning, not omitting
to pay attention to their order and numbers. As touching, indeed,
the real profundity of the matter, it seems to myself that I have
said very little, and that briefly and superficially" (PL 93.203AB).[33]

Bede does not list the *Octo quaestionum liber* in his catalogue of
exegetical works, but it has been attributed to him since the eighth
century and modern scholars have convincingly demonstrated that
it is his.[34] This indicates that in all probability it was composed
after he wrote the list in 731. The eight questions concern such
matters as the nature and significance of the star and the magi (qu.
1, PL 93.455–56), whether Paul's words "By night and by day I
was in the depth of the sea" (2 Cor. 11:25) should be understood
literally (yes) and what it signifies for us (the Lord will save us from
the depths of temptation, sin, and death) (qu. 3, 456–57).

Biblical Aids

In the *Ecclesiastical History* (V. 15) Bede speaks of the *De locis sanctis*
by the Irish abbot of Iona, Adamnan, based on information given
the abbot by Bishop Arculf, who had been a studious pilgrim in
the Holy Land. In chapters 16 and 17 Bede presents extracts from
it. Actually, Bede quotes from his own abridgment of Adamnan's
work, into which he incorporated some descriptions from Eucherius's
account of Jerusalem and Judaea and also from Hegesippus's adaption
of Josephus's *History of the Jews.* He speaks of his epitome at the

end of chapter 17: "If anyone wishes to know more of [Adamnan's] book, he may find it in the volume itself or in the abridgement of it which I have lately made" (pp. 512–13). He does not list the work again at the end of the book with his other works; perhaps he thought that this one mention should suffice or that the little work was not enough his work to call his own. The fact is, without a word of complaint he has notably improved on Adamnan's peculiar prose. In any case he again acknowledges his indebtedness to Adamnan in the epilogue to his version of *De locis sanctis* (CCSL 175, pp. 279–80).[35]

Bede also appended to two of his works gazetteers for locating and explaining places mentioned in the Bible. The first, *Nomina locorum ex beati Hieronimi presbiteri et Flavi Iosephi collecta opusculis,* is as the title states, a compendium garnered from the writings of Jerome and Flavius Josephus. It appears as a sequel to *In primam partem Samuhelis* (CCSL 119, pp. 273–87). The second, also quite likely genuine, is a geographical dictionary briefly explaining the names and places that appear in the Acts of the Apostles: *Nomina regionum atque locorum de Actibus Apostolorum.* It is found attached to the commentaries on Acts.[36] A modern reader may well expect to encounter esoteric names such as Mysia and Seleucia but will probably be amused to find an entry such as this: "Theater (Acts 19.29): a place borrowing a word from viewing, because in it the people standing and looking down from above viewed dramatic scenes." The necessity for such a gloss indicates how far removed the English monastic medieval world was from late antique secular Roman culture. It also indicates Bede's knowledge of Greek etymology.

Chapter Four
Homilies, Hagiography, Poems, Letters

These popular medieval genres, once dismissed as dull or derivative, have peculiar qualities that have elicited a good deal of interest and study in recent years. But, despite Bede's important contributions and fame in each of these categories, his own creations have received little theological, historical, or literary attention. Bede's writing was often praised in his age and is esteemed in ours for its clarity, cleanness, straightforwardness, and force.[1] Yet there has not yet been any comprehensive investigation into the sources of his style or any extensive study of the style itself.[2] Similarly, the other literary qualities the works possess have with few exceptions only been alluded to. At present relatively few students learn and become competent in Latin and particularly in postclassical Latin, so the laborers in this fruitful vineyard are scarce. Still, now that we have better editions of Bede, we may hope the literary neglect of his work, so immensely popular and influential in the early Middle Ages, will be remedied by dedicated and intelligent scholars.

The Homilies

"Homilies on the Gospel: two books" (*HE* V.24, pp. 568–69). For Bede, preaching as a form of teaching the meaning of Scripture, correct theological understanding, and moral rectitude had a special, even sacramental, significance. According to his view, preachers are the successors of the prophets and apostles.[3] Bede considered preaching the primary function of a priest: "spiritual pastors are especially ordained for this, that they preach the mysteries of the word of God, and the wonders that they have learned in the Scriptures they should display to their hearers to be wondered at" (I.7, CCSL 122, p. 49, ll. 100–4; see also p. 281). As a priest Bede took that function seriously indeed, as his collection of sermons on the Gospels, renowned and used widely throughout the Middle Ages, demonstrates. Many more sermons were attributed to Bede over the course of the Middle Ages than he authored. Further, many sermons were made by simply excerpting sections from his commentaries, especially on Mark and Luke, and assigning them to the Sundays when the gospel texts occur in the liturgy. Finally, the homilies that were his were transferred to different days to accommodate them to the later liturgy. The fact is, Bede composed fifty homilies, in two books of twenty-five each, ordered in the sequence of major feasts and Sundays of the liturgical year according to the Romano-Neapolitan use.[4] Since they are designed for general use (except for one that commemorates Benedict Biscop (*Homelia* I.13, CCSL 122, pp. 88–94), they provide few personal or local details about Bede and his immediate world; but they are clear indicators of Bede's religious attitudes and mature artistry. Although individual pieces may have come from an earlier period, he most likely assembled the collection between 730 and 735.

Bede's method of preaching is not greatly different from his exegetical procedure; that is, he takes the assigned gospel text for the day's feast and probingly comments on its verses, extracting its meanings, for the edification of the attentive Christian. It is a meditative process of rumination, savoring the spiritual content.[5] Since his sermons are essentially reflective, with the purpose of meditation on the divine mysteries, interior compunction, and quiet attainment of virtue, they differ from the public sermons of the Fathers. As usual he borrows pertinent parts from their works,[6] but he transforms them all into his monastic modality. His homilies do not display the rhetorical and oratorical flights of Ambrose's sermons to his Milanese church. They do not exhibit the pyrotechnics and rhetorical verve of Augustine's *Enarrationes in Psalmos,* preached to a noisy African congregation. They do not even directly resemble the papal sermons of Gregory the Great, though Gregory's attitudes and spirituality Bede greatly admired and imitated. They do posses their own splendid qualities of clarity, sincerity, and sobriety; they are also inventive. They remind one of the complex simplicity of Gregorian chant, in contrast to the bravura of a polyphonic orchestrated chorale.

Granted that Bede's homilies resemble the commentaries in general tone and technique, within the limits set for them they show a considerable range of artful diversity.[7] Sermons for the great high feast days of joy — Christmas, Easter, Pentecost—display more overall shape, structural symmetry, figures of speech, cadenced endings, liturgical formulae, and a higher style. Homilies for vigils, Advent, and Lent display a simpler mode, and a more verse-by-verse approach.

Even for the more austere occasions, however, there is no lack of artistry. Take, for a random example, homily II.14 for Rogation Days (or Greater Litanies), *In litaniis maioribus* (pp. 273–79). The Gospel for the day is Luke 11:9–13, in which Jesus says:

> I tell you, Ask, and it will be given you; seek, and you will find; knock, and it will be opened to you. For every one who asks receives, and he who seeks finds, and to him who knocks it will be opened. What father among you, if his son asks for a fish, will instead of a fish give him a serpent; or if he asks for an egg, will give him a scorpion? If you then, who are evil, know how to give good gifts to your children, how much more will the heavenly Father give the Holy Spirit to those who ask him?

After introducing the general intention of the text, Bede explains that "asking" refers to our praying, "seeking" describes right living, and "knocking" means our persevering. He develops the semantic fields of asking, seeking, and knocking for thirty lines. Then with a series of *ipse/nos* phrases, he contrasts the healing power of the Lord with our diseased condition (ll. 46–64). Next he turns to the reliability of God's response to those "calling upon him in truth" (Ps. 144:18): "They call upon the Lord in truth who say in their praying what they do not contradict in their living" (ll. 71–73). (Surely that phrasing is worthy of Augustine.) He moves from the concept of those seeking the Lord in truth to their opposites, those who seek badly (James 4:3; p. 274, ll. 88–89). He succinctly describes the four types of those seeking badly with a phrase beginning *male petunt* followed by a slightly but pleasingly varied clause (*qui* 89, *qui* 97, *quia* 104, *et illi qui* 107), all neatly turned to exhortation and giving the section closure: "It is true that all these kinds of seekers in so far as they seek badly *(male petunt)* will not merit to receive; let us strive, beloved, to seek well and to be worthy of obtaining what we seek" (p. 275, ll. 123–25). He proceeds to the next verses in Luke (11–12). At the literal level he stresses the comparison between an earthly father and the heavenly Father, emphasizing the sublimer qualities of the latter. Then he takes up the figural meanings (*iuxta typicam intelligentiam,* 149) of bread (charity, as the principal spiritual food), of fish in the water (faith in the element of God and surrounded by the pressures of adverse surroundings), and of the egg (hope for the future). These are the goods we are to ask for of the Father (186). God will not give us hardness of heart (stone), allow the poison of infidelity (serpent), or encourage backsliding (the sting in the scorpion's rear). Bede concludes the homily by identifying the "good spirit" given by God in verse 13 with the Holy Spirit who comes with the seven gifts prophesied by Isaiah (11:2–3). The sermon ends on a confident note of encouragement and promise (ll. 258–69). The homily is not elaborately rhetorical, but it does use a number of tropes and figures in a quietly effective way; it is not structured like a classical oration but it does move forward effectively and cumulatively to a strong conclusion; it does not move the emotions wildly, but it exhorts warmly; it pleases.

Hagiography

"Also the histories of the saints: a book on the life and passion of St. Felix the confessor, which I put into prose from the metrical version of Paulinus; a book on the life and passion of St. Anastasius which was badly translated from the Greek by some ignorant person, which I have corrected as best I could, to clarify the meaning. I have also described the life of the holy father Cuthbert, monk and bishop, first in heroic verse and then in prose" (*HE* V.24, pp. 568–71).

Bede composed these pieces with the conviction shared by all Christians, that God has conferred virtues and superior gifts on certain men and women who have responded courageously to his special call. With Augustine, Bede believed that their lives were signs of the wonderful rule and love God exercised in his world. The miracles they performed in life and after death were revelations of God's power and his intervention in history. God's justice, blessing the good through the saint and punishing the wicked who have oppressed him or her, is manifest in a fallen world in which injustice and suffering are the usual human experience.

Bede also understood well and carefully incorporated the literary conventions that had been established traditionally for the description of those saints' lives.[8] In this genre, the saint's career had to conform to accepted essential patterns and be characterized by a set of standard deeds that served as credentials and proof of divinely inspired life. Moral qualities, not individual characteristics, were paramount.

The story could be expressed in prose or poetry, or transferred from prose into poetry or vice versa. Bede exercised his talents in both forms. While discussing Aldhelm's works he calls the dual format *opus geminatum* (*HE* V.18).[9] It represents a development of the classical training program of *conversio,* paraphrase, an exercise of turning prose into poetry and vice versa. Prudentius, Juvencus, Caelius Sedulius, Arator, and Venantius Fortunatus developed the practice in Christian Latin literature. Although Aldhelm's prose version of *De virginitate* is more difficult than his poetic rendition, Bede and Alcuin used prose to provide accessibility and clarity, poetry to provide artifice and grandeur. A straightforward prose account could be read aloud to the community and be more or less understood at a first reading. It served to edify the simple as well as the learned. A simple style, with the use of direct quotation and unobtrusive rhetoric, was the norm. But a higher style, in poetic form, was used as panegyric for the saint.

For the *Vita Felicis* Bede paraphrased in chaste prose the ornate poetic version of the life and miracles of the third-century saint, Felix of Nola.[10] Writing quite early in his career, probably before 709, Bede explains what he has done to his source, the series of panegyrics by Paulinus of Nola (353–431) celebrating the *Natalicia* (that is, the birthday into heaven, 14 January) of Felix: "The most felicitous triumph of blessed Felix, which he merited with God's help in the Campanian city of Nola, the bishop Paulinus of that same city has described most beautifully and fully in hexameter verses. Because they are fitting for those versed in metrics rather than for simple readers, for the benefit of the many it has pleased me to elucidate the account with plainer words and to imitate the industry of the author who translated the martyrdom of blessed Cassian from the metrical work of Prudentius into common and suitable speech" (PL 94.789B).

Comparing Bede's clean, short, easily readable prose version with the elaborately florid poetic panegyrics of Paulinus is very instructive.[11] Although Bede picks up some of Paulinus's wordplay, especially at the beginning and end on the name Felix, the relatively simple structure, short sentences, uncomplicated syntax, and prosaic vocabulary of his text make it suitable for reading aloud to the monks in chapter or refectory.[12]

Why did Bede take the trouble to rewrite a life of this particular southern Italian saint? First, the cult of Saint Felix is part of the southern Italian influence on the Anglo-Saxon liturgy, much of it under the aegis of Hadrian when he became prior of Saint Peter's (later, Saint Augustine's) at Canterbury.[13] Other evidence of this influence includes Bede's ordering his homilies according to the Roman-Neapolitan tradition, the southern Italian features of books produced in the Wearmouth-Jarrow scriptorium, particularly its Bibles (the pandects), and the Bedan testimonies to the cultural influences of Theodore and Hadrian in the *Ecclesiastical History*. Second, as with his educational tracts and his exegetical commentaries, Bede is filling another gap in the Northumbrian Christian cultural void. Finally, this little life, a successful exercise in transfer from poetry to prose, is a charming and entertaining narrative, with its tale of Felix's using physical and verbal stratagems to elude the pursuing Romans, of stolen cattle finding their way home to a grieving old man by the intervention of Felix, of uncooperative tenants refusing to move their shabby dwellings and belongings from the immediate vicinity of Paulinus's elegant chapel for Felix.

Bede reworked a badly written life and passion of Saint Anastasius, the Persian monk martyred in 628 by Chosroes II. His relics were honored in Rome, and his cult was probably brought to England by Theodore and Hadrian (again that southern Italian connection). Until recently, Bede's version of the life of Saint Anastasius was considered lost. Now it seems that we possess not only the version "badly translated from the Greek by some ignorant person" but perhaps also Bede's own revision of it.[14] We have editions of the original Greek version of Anastasius's life and martyrdom. The slavish and awkward Latin translation, which Bede justifiably but rather peevishly criticizes (Bede was a man of standards), has come down to us in a single tenth-century manuscript witness, MS F.III.16 of the Biblioteca Nazionale of Turin, from the monastery of Bobbio. Most remarkably, according to the preliminary but painstaking analysis by Carmela Franklin and Paul Meyvaert, the version of BHL 408 may very likely be Bede's: the careful revision with respect for the integrity of the text, the aim to make sense of everything in the original, and the clean and orderly prose, all suggest Bede's

work. On the other hand, the manuscript tradition does not attribute
BHL 408 to Bede, and there are a few minor discrepancies between
the wording of his *Chronicle* and that of BHL 408. Since his version
was only a correction and not a total recasting of the life and passion
of Saint Anastasius, Bede may not have claimed or been assigned
authorship; moreover, the discrepancies between the life and chronicle entry are minor enough to be argued away.[15] Still, only more
research can lead to a firmer decision about the identity of the reviser.

Bede's most important hagiographic writing is an *opus geminatum*
on the life of Northumbria's great ascetic, Saint Cuthbert (ca. 634–
87), successively monk, recluse, and bishop of Lindisfarne. Both
Bede's versions represent a thorough reworking of an earlier (between
699 and 705) anonymous prose life by a brother or "brothers of the
church of Lindisfarne" (*HE* prologue, pp. 6–7). The anonymous
life is not without its virtues; as a matter of fact, some eminent
Bedan admirers—Plummer, Colgrave, Levison, Jones—have preferred it in some major ways to his versions.[16] Despite its wholesale
borrowings from the *Epistola Victorii Aquitani ad Hilarium,* Athan-
asius's *Vita Antonii,* Sulpicius Severus's *Vita sancti Martini,* and the
Actus Silvestri in the first sections, and despite its obvious use of
motifs from hagiographic lore, specifically Celtic, the four books of
the anonymous *vita* present a fairly detailed but quick-moving narrative of Cuthbert's life.[17] It possesses simplicity and spriteliness;
its strained attempts to relate the saint's actions to those of prominent types in the Bible are winsome. Indeed, its unsophisticated
freshness and spareness does contrast both with Bede's artifical and
learned poetic panegyric and with his carefully structured, stylistically superior, and generically more suitable prose account. The
criticism directed against Bede's versions seems to stem from a
misunderstanding of medieval literary genre and Bede's objective
for these works. The metrical version represents the same kind of
literary exercise that Juvencus and Sedulius performed on the Gospels
by transforming the humble prose account into highly stylized hexameter verse, the same kind of artistic heightening that hymnists
did for the liturgy, and that Christian men of letters such as Augustine sanctioned as a means of glorifying God.[18] The prose version,
on the other hand, served another purpose. Bede's words in the
preface to Bishop Eadfrith and the congregation of monks at Lindisfarne clearly intimate that he has been commissioned by them
to write an official life of the recent saint whose fame and cult, no

longer only familiarly local, had become widespread. As the best writer around, he accepted the task of writing the life and miracles of the saint in a form acceptable for *lectio divina,* for perusing not only in private devotion but also for annual public reading on the feast of the saint. He therefore took the anonymous Lindisfarne life as the most reliable textual history of Cuthbert's life and added to that his own findings from witnesses, particularly Herefrith. In order to improve the style of his source, he completely rewrote the life in his own lucid fashion, rearranging the sequence of events, smoothing transitions, adding quotations and augmenting plot to form a continuous narrative. By drawing out the spiritual and moral lessons to be derived from hagiographic reading, he observed the requirements of the genre. As J. F. Webb points out, "His main aim was not historical accuracy but imaginative truth within the framework of a conventional literary form, the saint's life."[19]

Bede wrote the metrical version of 979 competent hexameter lines between 705 and 716, according to the reference to Osred's reign in verses 552–55.[20] In the dedicatory preface Bede tells the priest John that he was unable to include all Cuthbert's wondrous deeds because new ones were daily being done through his relics and old ones were newly being brought to light. He then adds the striking comment: "One of those wondrous deeds I myself experienced by a guidance [or: curing] of the tongue *(per linguae curationem),* as I have already told you, while I was singing his miracles" (*Vita Cuthberti,* ed. Jaager, p. 57, ll. 17–19). Whether this means that Bede received direction and guidance through Cuthbert's inspiration as a saintly muse or whether he was cured of some lingual affliction is unclear because the Latin bears both meanings, "administration, attention, treatment, guidance," or "cure, healing," but modern critics favor the former.[21]

As the *apparatus criticus* of Jaager's edition makes clear, Bede's metrical version owes very little to the wording of the anonymous life, but it does remain closer to the order and arrangment of that source than does the prose version. Bede includes all miracles of the anonymous life except those only summarily mentioned without detail. And Bede adds a dozen chapters' worth of material.[22] But his poetic version provides less historical detail than the anonymous and certainly less than his prose version; in the former he placed greater emphasis on Cuthbert's wonders. Stylistically the poem follows the late antique classical tradition of Juvencus, Sedulius, and

Arator, from whom Bede takes phrases and vocabulary; but he also
uses Virgil copiously, and (according to the editor Jaager's conservative reckoning) in descending order of frequency, Cyprianus Gal-
lus, Venantius Fortunatus, Paulinus of Nola, Dracontius, Prudentius,
Aldhelm, Paulinus of Périgueux, Alcimus Avitus, Damasus, Serenus
Sammonicus, Ovid, Horace, Prosper, Orientius, Augustine, and
Persius. His metrics and prosody are enviably correct despite an
occasional variation from classical usage; he uses rhyme and allit-
eration sparingly (indicating how little Bede carries over the Anglo-
Saxon poetic verse traditon into his Latin). For anyone familiar with
early medieval poetry the poem offers no great difficulty and considerable pleasure.

The proem is nicely constructed, moving from the general view
of the Lord's numerous and various saints as lights of the Church
to examples of individuals, who shine particularly for their own
locale—e.g., Peter and Paul for Rome, Cyprian for Africa, John
Chrysostom for Constantinople, and finally Cuthbert for the English. Thus, at the outset Bede places Cuthbert in a cosmic setting
as the patron of the English but honored universally. In the spirit
and with the world as audience, Bede presents in studied and solemn
verse the glorified Cuthbert. In contrast to the solemnity of the
proem and the gravity of the prophetic warning of the destruction
of the monastery (chap. 37), some of the account is charming, mock-
pastoral and mock-heroic. The amusing mixture of Virgilian bucolic
and epic verse in the following passage reveals not only Bede's
command of classical verse but also his sense of humor:[23]

XVII

Quique suis cupiens victum conquiere palmis
Incultum pertemptat humum proscindere ferro
Et sator edomitis anni spem credere glebis.
Dumque seges modico de semine surgeret ampla,
Tempus adest messis; rapidae sed forte volucres
Flaventes praedare senis nituntur aristas.
Talia qui placidus saevis praedonibus infit:
"Quid precor inlicito messem contingitis ausu,
Quae vestro sulcis non est inserta labore?
Pauperies an vestra meam transcendit, ut istud
Incurvam merito falcem mittatis in aequor?
Quod si forte deus iubet his instare rapinis,

Non veto; sin alias, vos finibus indite vestris."
Dixerat, et cessit mox plumea turba nec ultra
Militis audebat domini iam laedere iura.
Quin potius dulci pacis quasi foedere nexum
Unanimemque sui generis redamabat amicum,
Nam teneras ceu pastor oves hanc ipse regebat. (ll. 413–30)

(Desiring to get food by means of his own hands, he works to cut through
the uncultivated soil with iron tool; and as a sower he entrusts the hope
of the year in the tamed glebe. After an ample crop results from the bit
of seed, it is time for the reaping. However, by chance quick birds strive
to plunder the old man's golden ears of grain. Placid, he begins to speak
to the savage thieves: "Why, I beg you, do you reach with illicit daring
for the harvest, which was not planted in the rows by your labor? Or does
your poverty exceed mine, that you should send your curved scythe justly
into that plain? If perhaps God orders you to press on with this rapine,
I do not forbid. If otherwise, put yourselves in your own territories." He
had spoken, and immediately the plumed mob ceased and dared not further
violate now the laws of the soldier lord. Rather, it formed a bond with
him as by a sweet pact of peace, and loved him as a united friend of its
race, for he ruled this group as a pastor his tender sheep.)

The prose life owes very little to the metrical life but a great deal
to the anonymous. Forty miracles are related in this version; only
eight are not in the anonymous (Colgrave, *Two Lives,* p. 14). Bede
points out in the preface that he showed his notes to the monks of
Lindisfarne for their criticism. Additional fine material, such as
chapter 33, and his beautiful account of Cuthbert's death, related
in chapters 37–39, he owes as he says to Herefrith. In Bede's hands
the life displays a skillful blend of the Roman and Celtic ideal ways
of monastic life. This is fitting not only because the writer himself
owes so much to both traditions but because the hero Cuthbert was
according to both biographers an interlocking cornerstone for the
two modes of life. In many respects Cuthbert resembles the enter-
prising Irish ascetics and pilgrim monks in his heroic penitential
practices, his search for solitude, and his missionary activity. The
arrangements of his Lindisfarne discipline and the relationship of
bishop, abbot, and community reveal elements of both Irish and
continental monasticism, which Bede feels obliged to explain ("ne
aliquis miretur" ["lest anyone should marvel"], chap. 16, p. 206).[24]
Bede does not include the detail from the anonymous life, that as
prior Cuthbert instituted a rule "which we observe even to this day

along with the rule of St. Benedict" (III.1, pp. 95–97). In the death scene, however, which is totally absent in the anonymous life, Bede has Cuthbert command: "Have no communion with those who depart from the unity of the Catholic peace, either in not celebrating Easter at the proper time or in evil living" (chap. 39, pp. 284–85).

Each of the three versions of Cuthbert's life has its literary and hagiographic merits, but these attributes differ greatly. It is clear from manuscript history that Bede's prose life won the palm in the Middle Ages: extant are seven manuscripts of the anonymous version, nineteen of Bede's metrical version, and thirty-six complete manuscripts of the prose version, not counting two containing extracts only and evidence for many more lost ones.[25] Just as it would prove enlightening to compare the entirety of one of Bede's biblical commentaries with its major source or sources, so a comparison of the three lives tells a student much about Bede's qualities as an author of hagiography.[26] His works invite a closer comparative analysis.

"A martyrology of the festivals of the holy martyrs, in which I have diligently tried to note down all that I could find out about them, not only on what day, but also by what sort of combat and under what judge they overcame the world" (HE V.24, p. 571). Besides the four saints' lives, Bede made another major contribution to hagiography. Using the pseudo-Jerome martyrology, a simple liturgical calendar naming the martyrs and the places of their martyrdom, Bede composed between 725 and 731 what is termed an historical martyrology, which includes a brief account of each saint's life and death. As the above quotation suggests, Bede did a great deal of research for this project, and, once again, the work is witness to an impressive number of sources, including some fifty lives of saints, ecclesiastical histories, writings of Fathers of the Church, and the Liber pontificalis.[27] A typical entry is that for Saint Cassian (the martyr, not the monk) on 13 August:

On the Ides of August. The birthday [into heaven] of St. Cassian, at Rome. When he had refused to adore idols, the persecutor demanded to know what his profession was. He answered that he taught students grammar (notas). Then, stripped of his clothes and bound with his hands behind his back, he was placed in the center. The boys to whom by his teaching he had become hateful were called, and permission was given them to destroy him. In so far as they suffered while learning, to that degree they enjoyed vengeance. Some beat him with their tablets and boards, others wounded him with their pens. In as much as their hands were weak, so much heavier, by an extended death, was the pain of his martyrdom. Prudentius the poet has written the life. (Quentin, p. 68; Dubois and Renaud, p. 149)

Bede's martyrology contained 114 notices. This left a number of calendrical spaces open. With the medieval *horror vacui,* later less careful, more sensational-minded editors encrusted Bede's work beyond recognition with their supplemental entries.[28]

Poems

> A book of hymns in various meters and rhythms.
> A book of epigrams in heroic and elegiac meter.
> (*HE,* V.24, pp. 570–71)

It seems that these two books did not survive the Middle Ages,[29] although a number of individual poems have come down to us. Besides the metrical life of Saint Cuthbert in almost a thousand lines of skillfully wrought hexameters, we have approximately two dozen poems of varying length and meter, some certainly by Bede and the rest quite probably so.

One poem, in honor of Saint Æthelthryth, we know is genuine because Bede includes it in the *Ecclesiastical History* (IV.20, pp. 396–401), with the introductory remark: "It seems fitting to insert in this history a hymn on the subject of virginity which I composed many years ago in elegiac meter in honor of this queen and bride of Christ, and therefore truly a queen because the bride of Christ; imitating the method of holy Scripture in which many songs are inserted into the account and, as is well known, these are composed in meter and verse."

> Alma Deus Trinitas, quae saecula cuncta gubernas
>   adnue iam coeptis, alma Deus Trinitas.
> Bella Maro resonet; nos pacis dona canamus,
>   munera nos Christi; bella Maro resonet.
> Carmina casta mihi, fedae non raptus Helenae
>   luxus erit lubricis, carmina casta mihi.

(All-bounteous Three in One, Lord of all time,
　Bless mine emprise, all-bounteous Three in One.
Battle be Maro's theme, sweet peace be mine;
　Christ's gifts for me, battle be Maro's theme.
Chaste is my song, not wanton Helen's rape.
Leave lewdness to the lewd! Chaste is my song.)

From this sample of the beginning lines, which bravely restate
the topos of the "contrast between pagan and Christian poetry,"
it is evident that the poem is something of a tour de force; it is not
only alphabetic (twenty-three distichs each beginning with another
letter, plus four for AMEN) but also epanaleptic (that is, the last
quarter of the distich repeats the first; termed in the Middle Ages
reciprocal, echoic, or serpentine).[30]

Unfortunately, the most recent edition by J. Fraipont in CCSL
122 of most of the rest of the poetry attributed to Bede has serious
defects.[31] Fraipont's edition goes by the title "Bedae Venerabilis
liber hymnorum, rhythmi, variae preces" (p. 405). This is misleading, since there are no "rhythmi" in the collection that accord
with Bede's definition from late Latin grammarians in his *De arte
metrica* I.24, where rhythmic poetry in contrast to metrical means
accentual verse.

Thirteen of the fifteen hymns taken by Fraipont from Dreves
1907 edition are probably by Bede; two, IV and V, are most probably
not, since they were never even attributed to him in the Middle
Ages.[32] Hymns I through XIII are in traditional Ambrosian hymn
meter, iambic dimeter.[33] Hymn I, *Primo Deus caeli globum,* is on a
topic dear to Bede's heart, as we have seen in his other works: the
six days of creation and the six ages of the world. After two introductory stanzas, the first line of one stanza becomes the last line of
the next, up to stanza 19, which, after the sabbath rest of souls on
the seventh day, deals with the extra-temporal eighth day of eternal
bliss. On that day and age,

> Vultumque Christi perpetim
> Iusti cernent amabilem
> Eruntque sicut angeli
> Caelesti in arce fulgidi.

(The just behold forever the lovable countenance of Christ; they will be
as shining angels in the celestial citadel.)

Stanza 28 ends the poem with a praise to the Trinity. Fraipont unaccountably includes the spurious stanzas 29 to 33, metrically defective and anticlimatic (pp. 410–11).

Hymn II, *Hymnum canentes martyrum,* is for the Feast of the Holy Innocents (28 December). Bede again uses the echoic stanza form, but here throughout the entire sixteen stanzas of the poem. Hymn IX, *In natali SS. Petri et Pauli,* another alphabetic poem, honors the two patron saints of Wearmouth and Jarrow.

Judging from the number of manuscripts extant, Hymn VI, *Hymnos canamus gloriae,* on the Ascension, was Bede's most popular.[34] The poem, with its emphasis on Christ's harrowing of hell and royal entrance into heaven, is an epitome of the early medieval theology of glory. It contains many of the scriptural and patristic motifs that will be used by Cynewulf in his Old English poem, *Christ II* or *The Ascension.*[35] After the beauty and regular meter of the first seventeen stanzas, the interpolated and defective stanza 17a spoils the flow, but 18 through 32 restores the reader's equilibrium.

Another hymn interesting because of its use of a device also found in Old English vernacular literature is the second hymn in honor of Saint Andrew, XIII, *Salue, tropaeum gloriae* (pp. 437–38). In this poem, the first seven stanzas are Andrew's address to the personified cross; they manifest Bede's literary debt to *The Passion of Saint Andrew the Apostle* and suggest some similarities to the prosopopoeia of *The Dream of the Rood.*[36]

A third poem, *De die iudicii* (XIV, pp. 439–44), is still more closely linked with the vernacular, since the fine Old English poem of the late tenth century, *Judgment Day II,* formerly called *Be Domes Dæge,* is a 304-line paraphrase of it.[37] The dactylic hexameter Latin poem, thought to have been composed between 716 and 731, is not in a usual sense a hymn, though it has been included in hymn collections, but a 163-line poem of meditation. Although the poem's authenticity has been questioned in the past, the evidence overwhelmingly supports Bedan authorship. Thirty of the thirty-nine extant manuscripts ascribe it to him; and it has been assigned to no other writer. In Northumbrian manuscripts the poem has a personal epilogue in lines 156 to 163 (p. 144) addressed to Bede's patron, Bishop Acca, and his monks at Hexham. The theme of doomsday is consonant with Bede's other writings, such as *De temporum ratione* (68–70) and Dryhthelm's account of his trip to the otherworld in *HE* V.12 (pp. 488–99). Nevertheless, Jean Mabillon's impression "it does not seem to follow Bede's vein" still finds adherents, especially since Bede does not elsewhere dwell so on physical pain and torment as depicted in lines 72 to 122 of the poem; in the commentary on Revelation he prefers to transfer such descriptions to an allegorical plane.[38] Still, in addition to the other evidence, it must be admitted that the competent hexameters, poetic but restrained diction, and clean style point to Bede as author. The subject matter of the poem, the separation of the just and unjust according to their merits, their rewards and punishment, naturally prompts a contrastive treatment, but this is done quite effectively. The poem starts out with a line describing a pleasant glade, using the classical and medieval topos of the *locus amoenus,* but immediately wheels about in the second line with a description of a powerful wind that brings on melancholy in line four. The earthly flowery scene in the first line parallels the rosy aspect of heaven in 146–47; the list of hell's sufferings, 93–97 (beginning "Nec uox ulla") contrasts exactly with heaven's joys, 124–28 (echoing with "Nox ubi nulla"). A careful reading of the poem renders F.J.E. Raby's dismissal of it highly contestable: "Its merits are small and it displays nothing half so well as the piety of its author."[39]

Poem XV, *Oratio Bedae Presbyteri,* is a twenty-six line prayer in elegiac·couplets. XVI, XVII, and XVIII are poems based on Psalms 41, 83, and 112.

Occasionally Bede inserted a brief poem, epigram, or epitaph before, in, or after a prose work.[40] We apparently also now have some remnants of his lost *Liber epigrammatum.* John Leland, commissioned by Henry VIII to search out British antiquities in ecclesiastical libraries, relates in his *Collectanea* that he inspected a very old collection of epigrams (the manuscript is now lost) belonging to Milred (bishop of Worcester from 745–75), five of which were attributed to Bede apparently on good grounds; Leland transcribed two of them, which Michael Lapidge has recently published and discussed.[41] The last, acephalous epigram in Milred's collection may also be from the concluding lines of Bede's book.[42]

We have Bede's own authority and that of his contemporary Cuthbert that he translated Latin into Old English (Letter to Cuthbert, *EHD* I, p. 801; Letter on the Death of Bede, *HE,* pp. 582–83), and Cuthbert also says that Bede was versed in Old English poetry (Letter, pp. 580–81). Furthermore, from his account of Cædmon's poetic gift and career in *HE* IV.24, (pp. 414–21), we know that Bede was sensitive to the beauty and uniqueness of Old English verse and acknowledged it as a medium for translating and embellishing the sacred text. But there is no compelling evidence that he composed the five-line poem called "Bede's Death Song." The evidence of the early and best manuscripts of Cuthbert's letter indicates only that Bede repeated the little poem as a favorite during his last days. Cuthbert's words are: "In nostra quoque lingua, ut erat doctus in nostris carminibus, dicens de terribili exitu animarum et corpore" ("And in our own language,—for he was familiar with English poetry,—speaking of the soul's dread departure from the body, he would repeat:

> Fore ðæm nedfere   nænig wiorðe
> ðonc snottora   ðon him ðearf siæ
> to ymbhycgenne   ær his hinionge
> hwæt his gastæ   godes oððe yfles
> æfter deað dæge   doemed wiorðe.

> (Facing that enforced journey, no man can be
> More prudent than he has good call to be,
> If he consider, before his going hence,
> What for his spirit of good hap or of evil
> After his day of death shall be determined.)
> (*HE,* pp. 580–83)[43]

Letters

"Also a book of letters to various people: one of these is on the six ages of the world; one on the resting-places of the children of Israel; one on the words of Isaiah, 'And they shall be shut up in the prison, and after many days shall they be visited'; one on the reason for leap year; and one on the equinox, after Anatolius" (*HE* V.24, pp. 568–69).

From this epistolary catalogue it is obvious that Bede did not will to posterity a collection of warm and familiar letters. Although the book itself has not come down to us as such, we have all the five letters listed, in addition to two others, written after the *Ecclesiastical History* was finished.

The first letter (CCSL 123C, pp. 617–26), on the six ages, was discussed in connection with the *De temporibus* above in Chapter 2. Addressed to Plegwin, monk of Hexham, Bede responds heatedly to the charge of heresy for his reckonings concerning the time span of the ages and Christ's birth in the sixth age; he refutes the accusations laid against him at Bishop Wilfrid's feast and asks that "the most learned brother David" set things straight.[44]

The last two letters listed (four and five) also deal with computation questions put to Bede by colleagues, but in less controversial areas. After removing the paragraph of salutation addressed to Helmwald (printed in CCSL 123C, p. 629), Bede makes the verbatim text of the fourth letter serve as chapters 38–39 of *De temporum ratione* (CCSL 123B, pp. 399–404) to explain bissextile (leap year) intercalation (see above, Chap. 2). The fifth, the letter to Wicthed (CCSL 123C, pp. 633–42), wrestles with problems about the vernal equinox for the dating of Easter in the Anatolian *Canon* and serves as sort of an appendix to the treatment of equinoxes in *De temporum ratione* (see Chap. 2).

The second and third letters respond to questions of exegesis asked by Bede's patron, Bishop Acca, for whom he wrote so much. Bede interrupted his commentary on 1 Samuel to compose the letters (PL 94.699A and 702B). They are like the *Eight Questions* discussed in Chapter 3 in that they take a particular biblical topic and discuss it discursively rather than by Bede's usual method of verse-by-verse commentary. *De mansionibus* enumerates and describes the Israelites' stopping places in Exodus and then, following Jerome's interpretation, explains the allegorical, moral meaning of those resting areas (701C–D). The third letter deals with a harder nut, Isaiah 24:22, which seems to prophesy a punishment in hell that will end, since the Vulgate texts says, "they will be visited" (not "they will be punished" [RSV]). The latter part of this long letter discusses the apocalyptic visitation of the Antichrist.

Along with a copy of the recently completed *Ecclesiastical History,* Bede sent a short letter of appreciation to Albinus, abbot of the monastery of Saints Peter and Paul at Canterbury (Plummer I, p. 3).[45] In the preface to the *Ecclesiastical History* Bede recognizes Albinus as "the principal authority and helper" in the historical enterprise by his generous provision of documents from Canterbury and Rome (*HE,* pp. 3–4). In conjunction with the information contained in the preface to the *History* and in the prologue to the life of Saint Cuthbert, this letter tells us something of Bede's publishing procedures: he sent out drafts *(schedulae)* for verification and correction, then a fair copy *(membranulae)* for final approval and copying. Since the manuscript was publicized and copied in various degrees of revision, different versions, or editions, naturally ensued.[46]

The last letter and the last surviving work of Bede is also the most critical of church and state. It is a letter calling for reform. Although all the principal works of his late years deal to some extent with reform of church, to be brought about by a rejuvenated monasticism and episcopate, and reform of society, to be brought about by a well-counseled king and advisors, Bede spells out in detail what a program should entail.[47] On 5 November 734 Bede writes to Ecgbert, who would be elevated as the first archbishop of York in 735, and whose brother Eadbert would become king of Northumbria in 737 (*EHD* I, pp. 799–810; Plummer I, pp. 405–23; II, pp. 378–88). Though in weakened condition physically, Bede energetically admonishes the prelate to carry out much-needed reforms. The tone is that of a prophet exhorting a high priest, and may remind us of another monk, Bernard of Clairvaux, reproving the pope. Actually, this seems to be an early instance of a traditional Christian genre called the *sermo ad clerum,* an admonition to the hierarchy by a respected but lesser ranking member of the clerical club, a convention familiar to students of the English Renaissance in the sermons of Colet and Latimer.

Bede had complained of ecclesiastical abuses of his day in his commentaries and history,[48] but nowhere is he as detailed as he is in this outspoken letter. After calling attention to reports about bishops associating with "those who are given to laughter, jests, tales, feasting and drunkenness, and the other attractions of the lax life" (reminiscent of his censure of Bishop Wilfrid's court in his letter to Plegwin), he points out that the distances are too great in the diocese to serve all the people (p. 801). He notes with some bitterness "that many villages and hamlets of our people are situated on inaccessible mountains and dense woodlands, where there is never seen for many years at a time a bishop to exhibit any ministry or celestial grace; not one man of which, however, is immune from rendering dues to the bishop" (p. 802). He therefore recommends that new bishoprics be established, with sees established and financed at wealthy monasteries. Pseudo-monasteries, set up as personal familial institutions to acquire lands held by hereditary title by royal indult, to evade taxes, and to avoid public service, he entreats be abolished.[49]

For—what indeed is disgraceful to tell—those who are totally ignorant of the monastic life have received under their control so many places in the name of monasteries, as you yourself know better than I, that there is a complete lack of places where the sons of nobles or of veteran thegns can receive an estate. . . . But others give money to kings, and under the pretext of founding monasties buy lands on which they may more freely devote themselves to lust, and in addition cause them to be ascribed to them by hereditary right by royal edicts, and even get those same documents of their privileges confirmed, as if in truth worthy of God, by the subscription of bishops, abbots and secular persons. (p. 805)

This sour complaint serves as an interesting complement to the description in the *Historia ecclesiastica* (V.23): "In these favorable times of peace and prosperity, many of the Northumbrian race, both noble and simple, have laid aside their weapons and taken the tonsure, preferring that they and their children should take monastic vows rather than train themselves in the art of war. What the result will be, a later generation will discover" (pp. 560–61).

Although this statement seems either contradictory or ironically cynical when placed against the text of his letter to Ecgbert, Bede is actually expressing the complex state of affairs in contemporary Northumbria, where the presence of the church is hearteningly affirmed by dedication of lives and land to its service, but also where the quality of the church is seriously vitiated by greed, subterfuge, and fraud. What saves the letter from querulousness are its positive recommendations with a true hope of improvement.[50]

After pleading for adequate spiritual teachers for the laity, Bede ends the letter with a fervent appeal that Ecgbert avoid avarice, remembering its effects on religious leaders in the Old and New Testaments (pp.809–10). Bede's swan song is a strong and urgent cry.[51]

Chapter Five
The Histories

Bede's fame today derives mainly from his work as an historian. Although he was renowned throughout the Middle Ages as an exegete and indeed spent most of his career commenting voluminously on Scripture, his principal modern reputation as an historian is not unjustified. Medieval Biblical exegesis would have survived intact without Bede, but without Bede medieval English history would not have. His histories not only provide us with data now known only because of him; they also mark momentous advances in the science of historiography. They are products of his mature scholarship and long writing career—the *Ecclesiastical History of the English People* is his last major work. All his education, training, and talent culminate in that *History*. In it, his unitary program of monastic culture comes to final fruition. In it, his reforming idealism, expressed earlier in his hagiographic portrait of Saint Cuthbert, and his monastic vision of sacred and secular history, as evident in his characterizations of the Northumbrian kings Edwin and Oswald, are combined. His many years as a teacher and writer of postclassical Latin, coupled with his impressive natural endowments, enabled him to write a beautifully structured, long but coherent, carefully styled treatise. His many years as an exegete had honed his interpretative skills; the commentaries on the Gospels and Acts had especially practised his talents for narrative, artistic selectivity, and reconciliation of real and seeming contradictions. His many years as a computist developed his special abilities for chronology, for reckoning calendrical time, for correcting mistakes and corrupt texts, and for understanding temporal sequence and relationships. His works of biography and hagiography had trained him to incorporate detail and sign into the larger fabric, to utilize reports, accounts, and miracle stories for studied effect. His expertise in poetry as well as prose allowed him free rein to use both forms to suit his purpose, and his epistolary exercises allowed him to edit and use letters effectively in his historical account. The fact that many of his works were digests, revisions, or summaries of earlier materials also served his formation as an historian. All his training as grammarian, exegete, literary artist, and chronologer was brought to bear on history. Conversely, his historical work boldly and candidly manifests the means and ends of each of those disciplines, so that literature and its devices, hermeneutics in both its literal and allegorical manifestations, saints' lives and miracles, and modes of ecclesiastical and secular history are all represented and melded.

The Lives of the Abbots of Wearmouth and Jarrow

"A history of the abbots of this monastery in which it is my joy to serve God, namely Benedict, Ceolfrith, and Hwætberht, in two books" (*HE* V.24, pp. 570–71).

As in his saints' lives, Bede's account of the lives of the first abbots of Wearmouth-Jarrow had in part a previously written source. In this case, the *Life of Ceolfrith* (also known as the *Historia abbatum auctore anonymo*, even though it is principally about Ceolfrith) was no mean prototype. The style, method, and theme strongly suggest that Bede himself was the author; he may have omitted it in his list of writings because he considered it a preliminary version of the more extensive *Lives of the Abbots*.[1] A well-written history in thirty-nine brief chapters, it contains invaluable data about the Northumbrian monastery and its leader and describes the internal workings of the monastery and its cultural relationships with Gaul and Rome. It is straightforwardly historical, delaying any account of miraculous wonders until the apparitions at Ceolfrith's tomb related at the end of the last chapter. The author is fond of archival documentation and is careful about dating, indicating events by the regnal years of the Northumbrian kings, or by indictions, or by the year of the Incarnation. In the latter usage, which appears in English annals on a regular basis throughout the seventh century,[2] this history antedates Bede's *Ecclesiastical History* (though Bede had already used it in his books on time and it was because of Bede's popularity that dating according to B.C. and A.D. eventually became universal in Europe).

Bede quotes from the anonymous life in the chronicle he attaches to the end of *De temporum ratione*, rather than from his own history of the abbots. This indicates that his own history of the abbots postdates both the anonymous life and his chronicle.

Besides freely incorporating and editing this anonymous life of Ceolfrith into his *History of the Abbots of Wearmouth and Jarrow*, Bede adds items of traditional material and personal experience. Bede appends as book I (chaps. 1–14), the life and career of the great founder of his monastery, Benedict Biscop, which supplements his homiletic eulogy of that dynamic leader (*Homilia 13 in natali S. Benedicti Biscopi*, CCSL 122, pp. 88–94). Benedict, descended from noble lineage, "refused to become the father in the flesh of mortal children, being foreordained of Christ to bring up in spiritual learning immortal children for Him in the heavenly life" (*HA* chap. 1, Campbell, p. 372). In his journeys to Gaul and Rome "he brought back a large number of books relating to the whole of sacred learning" (*HA* chap. 4, p. 374; also chaps. 6, 9, 11) and other treasures for the monastery he founded under King Ecgfrith's auspices. After dealing with Benedict's life, especially these purposeful trips of piety and acquisition, Bede treats of his holy death and testament to his monks (*HA* chaps. 11–14, pp. 380–85). In this first part of the *History* he also interfuses the histories of Benedict's subordinate abbots, Ceolfrith, Eosterwine, and Sigefrith. The eighth chapter, a separate eulogy on Eosterwine, contains a particularly moving account of that nobleman's monastic humility. After a summary chapter of their lives (*HA* chap. 14), book II constitutes the revised history of Ceolfrith's reign, emphasizing Ceolfrith's own contributions ("he doubled the size of the library for both monasteries" [*HA* chap. 15, p. 385]) and piety (*HA* chap. 16, pp. 386–87) before discussing his resignation and elected replacement, Bede's coeval Hwætberht. The history ends with Ceolfrith's pious death at Langres on his way to Rome with the great Bible, the *Codex Amiatinus*, as a gift of homage to the pope.

Significantly, Bede attributes no miracles to any of the five holy abbots. This could be interpreted as Bede's honest reluctance to ascribe miracles to men whose lives he knew had caused none. But he omits even the modest account of the miraculous apparitions at Ceolfrith's tomb in the last chapter of the anonymous life. This points to an important generic difference between hagiology in Bede's saints' lives and in numerous chapters of the *Ecclesiastical History* and the history of an abbey. Bede's one venture into historical biography may anticipate the monastic local chronicle, widespread from the eleventh century on, which factually described the establishment, leadership, patronage, and possessions of a foundation.[3]

The Chronicles

The chronicle, as the briefest summary of major events, serves as a sort of historical index. It differs from the genre of history, which as a literary form has material arranged and developed according to a sustained theme. Both forms, chronicle and history, were bequeathed to the Middle Ages by Eusebius of Caesarea (c. 260–c. 340). Eusebius's *Chronicle*, based on the time scheme of the Septuagint, was translated intact by Jerome and followed blindly by Isidore. While generally following the Eusebian-Jerome version, Bede revised the time scheme (for which he was charged with heresy, as we noted in our discussion of the Letter to Plegwin, Chaps. 2 and 4).

Bede's two world chronicles (discussed in Chap. 2, as part of his educational treatises on time) very briefly note in chronological order the most important events in what was considered world (that is, Roman and ecclesiastical) history. Bede arranges the events within his favorite historical framework of the six ages, according to his own reckoning of time intervals indicated in the Vulgate Bible. The two chronicles display some major differences. The first, shorter chronicle attached to the *De temporibus* (CCSL 123C, pp. 601–11) only includes the structure of six ages and has a last entry of 703, whereas the longer, more developed chronicle at the end of the *De temporum ratione* (CCSL 123B, pp. 463–544), after its last entry for the year 725, has additional theological chapters on the end of the sixth age, the time of the second coming ("All his holy ones love with good cause the advent of the Lord and want it to be present rather soon; but they act dangerously if any presume to think or predict that this is near or far away" [chap. 68, p. 537, ll. 1–3]), the arrival of the Antichrist, and the seventh and eighth ages beyond time. To envisage how greatly expanded the second chronicle is over the first, compare the two as printed in parallel in Mommsen's edition (MGH, *Auctorum antiquissimorum* XIII.247–327). Although for dating the chronicles Bede uses the *annus mundi* (the year of the world according to Biblical reckoning from the Creation) and indictions (fifteen-year Roman cycles), in the paschal tables of both treatises on time to which the chronicles are attached he uses the dating of *anno Domini*. His source for the A.D. dating is clear: at the entry for the year 518 (p. 521, ll. 1717–18) of the second work we find, "Dionysius [Exiguus, died c. 527] composes the paschal cycles beginning from the Lord's incarnation." In the summary of British history dating from the attack of Julius Caesar provided at the end of the *Ecclesiastical History* (V.24, pp. 560–67), as for the dating within the history, Bede employs the A.D. method, which set the standard for all future histories.

Bede's chronicles influenced both the epitome appended to his *History* and the *Anglo-Saxon Chronicle*, both for the A.D. dating and for early recorded events, especially in the north. But the relationship of the *Anglo-Saxon Chronicle* to Bede's chronicles is a complex one.[4]

The Ecclesiastical History of the English People

"The history of the Church of our island and race, in five books" (*HE* V.24, pp. 570–71.)

With this brief entry Bede lists the work that established his eternal fame. His other works, large and small, have been neglected either by translators or by critics or by both to an extent surprising for the most renowned writer of his age. Only one of his biblical commentaries (on the seven Catholic Epistles) and one of his educational treatises (on figures and tropes) have been translated in print. The *History of the Abbots*, even though translated a half dozen times, has never received a full-length study. But the *Ecclesiastical History* is another matter. A multitude of manuscripts from the Middle Ages (over 150), both in England and on the Continent, indicate its renown.[5] Since the Renaissance it has been printed, edited (brilliantly by Smith in 1723, using the Moore manuscript, then by Plummer in 1896, and by Mynors with Colgrave in 1969, incorporating the Leningrad manuscript readings), translated, and commented upon numerous times. It constantly challenges leading contemporary medievalists to augment, revise, correct, or validate Plummer's commentary. The grounds for this interest are apparent to every serious student of the Middle Ages, even though the aspects of the *History* that appealed to readers of the past differ from those we find engaging.

The title of the work tells us what to expect from it. It is not like the classical histories of Herodotus, Thucydides, Livy, Caesar, or Tacitus; indeed, there is no evidence that Bede or his contemporaries even knew them. It is an "ecclesiastical history"; that is, it belongs in part to the genre and tradition established by Rufinus's translation of Eusebius's *Ecclesiastical History*.[6] An ecclesiastical his-

tory, based on biblical rather than classical concepts of time and
event, presupposes a theocentric universe in which primary concern
is focused on the sacred, and the secular is understood in terms of
the sacred; it is a history that traces the development of the church
as it advances in time and geography to "the ends of the earth"
(Acts 1:8). It describes conversion and the spread of the faith. But
because the accomplishment of that development in the sixth age
is to be accompanied by apocalyptic evils, such a history is not
naively cheery but only guardedly optimistic.

In technique as in content, ecclesiastical history differs from pagan
historiography, which frequently uses fiction to arrive at the author's
idea of truth. Although Bede's *Ecclesiastical History* is of another age
and possesses characteristics distinct from that of Eusebius, both
Eusebius and Bede include documents and give references to sources.

Bede's ecclesiastical history is "of the English people," as he states
in the preface (p. 2), and this marks it off from the universal history
of Eusebius. In this part of the title he signals his intention to record
the history of one nation, as Gregory of Tours did in the *History of
the Franks*. In his work Bede accomplishes an unprecedented synthesis of Eusebian historiography with local history that stands in
sharp contrast to Gregory's awkward and undigested record. In
showing that the English Church developed according to the Eusebian model, Bede is making the people of England, and especially
of his beloved Northumbria, one of God's chosen tribes. Bede was
always sensitive to the remoteness of his country geographically and
temporally from the Mediterranean centers of Christianity, Jerusalem and Rome; but he is asserting in his history that in these days
the converted English, "our people" (Letter to Albinus), are a tribe
of the new Israel even at the ends of the earth. Bede followed the
usage of Pope Gregory in referring to the whole people as "Angli"
rather than "Saxones." Even after Bede, many others, such as Boniface and Alcuin, preferred to call themselves Saxons, but Bede's
authority had established the nomenclature in perpetuity.[7]

The preface to the *History* is, like much of Bede, at once conventional and quite original. It is constructed of exordial topoi that
entered Christian historiography from classical literature: it addresses a leader with a formula of submission by which a subject
presents himself as a servant (*famulus*) seeking his benevolence, art-
fully intermixed with a devotional formula, *famulus Christi*.[8] Using

other topoi, it sets forth the moral usefulness of history; turning to the wider audience, it points to its reliable sources; it requests with authorial modesty the indulgence of the readers. Bede turns all these topoi to his own purpose and adapts them accordingly. First comes the dedication. The only work of Bede honoring a layman, Ceolwulf, king of Northumbria (729–37/8), the *History* is clearly intended for a lay as well as a clerical audience. The dedication to the prince presages one important thematic interest in the *History*, that of royal conduct.[9] It carefully records the succession and genealogy of kings. It is in part an early form of the mirror for princes, so prominent in the later Middle Ages and Renaissance. In his accounts of the careers of Æthelbert, Edwin, Saint Oswald, Oswiu, Oswine, Sigebert of the East Saxons, Cenwealh of Wessex, and others, Bede illustrates the role of Christian kings, to protect and defend their people and the Church, to observe its teachings, and to further its success. He shows how they prosper when observing Christian law and virtue, and how the Church avails them and they the Church.[10] The earthly power of Edwin and Oswald magnified after their conversion (II.9 and III.6), and Oswiu and Aldfrith because of their faith overpowered superior forces in war (III.24). Bede also provides negative examples of divine retribution for infidelity and backsliding. But Bede is a Christian monk who knows from the psalms and prophets that the wicked often prosper in this life as a test of faith and penance for sins, so the narrative of royal events is not naively or perversely skewed to fit a simple thesis of virtue immediately rewarded in this life. Virtue is not always to a king's earthly advantage. He gives us Saint Aidan's comment when King Oswine humbled himself before him: "I know the king will not live long; for I never before saw a humble king; therefore I think he will very soon be snatched from this life; for this nation does not deserve to have such a ruler" (III.14, pp. 258–59).

If Bede intended the *History* to serve at least in part as a *speculum principis* for King Ceolwulf and other Anglo-Saxon rulers, why did he write it in Latin, the language of the Church and not the layman? The answer in part is that Ceolwulf like his predecessor Aldfrith, whom Bede calls "most learned in all respects" (V.12, pp. 496–97), had obviously received Latin education. Bede sent advanced drafts of the *History* to both Albinus and Ceolwulf for their perusal and criticism. Furthermore, Ceolwulf retired as a monk to Lindisfarne in 737, after a reign "filled with so many and such serious commotions and setbacks" that Bede was unwilling as he finished the *History* to predict the results (V.23, pp 558–59).[11]

Another reason why Bede wrote the *Historia* in Latin is that it also, and in greater part, is directed to the clergy with hierarchical approval, as the correspondence with Abbot Albinus of Canterbury reveals. As an ecclesiastical history, it is in large measure about the clergy and their activity in the Church. It catalogues and discusses episcopal succession (II.3–9). It not only describes the work of saintly prelates such as Gregory the Great, Augustine of Canterbury, Paulinus, and Theodore, but also adroitly includes in a diffuse, neutralizing fashion the chequered career of Wilfrid. To a Church enjoying a status it would never surpass in learning, national apostolate, and missionary activity abroad, Bede offers the models of John of Hexham, Aidan, and Cuthbert. Indeed, the *History* climaxes in book IV.27–32 with the life and miracles of the last-named saint already eulogized by Bede in his prose life, a saint who was both monk and prelate, Irish in training but Roman in his respect for the Rule of Benedict and the reckoning of the date of Easter. Cuthbert stands as a model for the clergy as Oswald does for the lay leader.[12] True to his monastic and didactic vocation, Bede holds up the examples of good and bad behavior in the *History* as moral incentives for both cleric and layman (preface, pp. 2–3).

The greater part of the extensive preface is taken up with acknowledgment of sources (pp. 2–7). In this Bede goes far beyond the conventional appeal to compelling witnesses. As in his commentaries on the Gospels, and in remarkable contrast to the practice of other early medieval authors, Bede is here as in his biblical exegesis at pains to list his authorities with their credentials. Nevertheless, for the background information for the history of the Church in England, that is, for the period from the beginnings up to the arrival of Augustine, Bede only remarks that he got the "material from here and there, chiefly from the writings of earlier writers" (pp. 4–5). An analysis of chapters 1–22 of book I reveals that Bede put together this historical prelude somewhat like an encyclopedia article; it is a collection of neatly assembled quotations from late antique and British authors: Pliny, Solinus, Orosius, Eutropius, Vegetius, Basil, Prosper, the *Liber Pontificalis*, the lives of Saint Alban and of Saint Germanus, and especially Gildas.[13] For the period from the conversion to the present (particularly the recent past), Bede is more explicit about his sources of information. Such a procedure makes sense even to a modern reader: the preliminary material is treated as common knowledge; but the core of the history is verified by certified sources. These sources, written and oral, include: for Canterbury, Kent, and relations with Rome and with English sees, Abbot Albinus through the intermediary of Nothelm from London, who examined the archives in Rome as well; for the West Saxons, South Saxons, and Wight, Bishop Daniel; for Mercia and the East Saxons, the monks of Lastingham; for East Anglia, oral and written tradition and Abbot Esi; for Lindsey, Bishop Cyneberht and others; for Northumbria, "the faithful testimony of innumerable witnesses" and the lives (his own and the anonymous) of Saint Cuthbert. As Bede summarizes at the end of the *History* (V.24, pp. 566–67), the material was assembled "either from ancient documents or from tradition or from my own knowledge." But the result is totally his art. [14]

Bede concludes his summary of sources with a disarming plea: "I humbly implore the reader that he not impute it to me if in what I have written he finds anything other than the truth. For, in accordance with a true law of history [*uera lex historiae*], I have tried to set down in simple style what I have collected from common report, for the instruction of posterity." The loaded phrase, *uera lex historiae*, which Bede also used in his commentary on Luke 2:33––34 (CCSL 120, p. 67, ll. 1905–12), here means that, although he has tried to use only trustworthy data, he has of necessity had to rely on much oral tradition and hearsay for which he cannot be held unreasonably accountable; but the probable truth of the material urges its inclusion. [15]

In the last paragraph of the preface Bede points out that what he has recorded for the various areas should give pleasure to the inhabitants. This explains in part his frequent interspersion of story and anecdote in the *History*. But it is also clear from the architecture and narrative thrust of the *History* that the great aim of the whole work was to expound the development of God's plan for the English as a chosen people and the development of one unified Church in that violent and feuding land. It tells of the coming of the faith to a beautiful but remote island, of the failures among the Celts and the initial successes among the English, its progress and its setbacks, and its present position. [16]

The five books trace the history of England and the English

chronologically, except for some necessary displacements and back-tracking for historical narrative, thematic groupings, and concurrent events and personages of the different kingdoms. He deftly inserts short biographies into the chronological narrative, usually in the form of a summary memorial after recording the person's death. Although Bede, the most reliable and practiced chronographer of his age, strives for accuracy about dates, times, and events, he sometimes makes a mistake. He had to work with a vast quantity of unmanageable, lacunal, and discordant oral and written records, variously dated by memory and disparate regnal and indictional records. The marvel is that he got so much right and set so much straight. [17]

The first three books deal primarily with the Christianization of the English; the last two books describe the way in which the Christian life developed among them. Although each of the books is about equal in size, the first book sweeps through 650 years, whereas each of the remaining four covers about a generation. Historians have noticed, however, that Bede discusses the recent past much more completely and critically than his own, which he seems reluctant to explore, perhaps because he thought it too proximate to be judged properly. Each of the books and its parts manifest an artistic organizational symmetry. Besides ordering his material chronologically and geographically, Bede also arranges it in clusters by association with a certain person, place, or event. For instance, as Donald Fry has observed, "Bede's *Ecclesiastical History* contains fifty-one miracles, most of them grouped into clusters, usually around a person, such as Cuthbert, a subgenre, such as visions of hell, or a place, such as the double monastery at Barking." Within the clusters, Bede unifies by use of particular images and symbols. Thus in the Barking series (IV.7–11, pp. 356–69), he unifies by "complicated patterns of diction and imagery invoking light and fearful confinement." [18]

Book I first provides the geographical and historical background for the coming of the Anglo-Saxons, their arrival as mercenaries to assist the British and remaining as the Britons' masters (I.15), and the neglect on the part of the indigenous sinful Celts to convert them. [19] "Nevertheless God in his goodness did not reject the people whom he foreknew" (I.22, pp. 68–69), so Pope Gregory sent Augustine to win the English for Christ (I.23–26). The long chapter containing the purportedly verbatim responses of Gregory to Augustine's pastoral questions reveals Bede's respect for his documentary sources, especially by the ecclesiastical hero of the Anglo-Saxon Church, Pope Gregory; Bede does not correct even obvious grammatical errors in the Canterbury copy of the *Libellus responsionum*.[20]

Book I does not end with an account of the spread of Christianity in southeastern England and the deaths of the first archbishop of Canterbury, Augustine, and his first abbot, Peter (chap. 33); rather, it concludes with a chapter on the career of the pagan king, Æthelfrith of Northumbria (chap. 34). Through its exultant tone, which comes close to the bravura of *The Battle of Brunanburh*, and through its biblical allusion to King Saul, ("but with this exception, that Æthelfrith was ignorant of the divine religion"), the chapter combines the Old Testament militarism of the Book of Joshua and the Old English heroic boast: "No ruler or king had subjected more land to the English race or settled it, having first exterminated or conquered the natives." It concludes with the vaunt, "From that time no Irish king in Britain has dared to make war on the English race to this day" (pp. 116–17).[21] The book thus comes to a close with both the initial spiritual conquest of the English by the missionaries and the physical overthrow of the Irish, one of the Celtic enemies in the west, by a Northumbrian king, anticipating the Northumbrian history in the next books.

In the first chapter of book II, at the end of the short biography of Gregory the Great done in loving tribute to that monastic pope for his service to the English Church, Bede cannot resist adding the legend about the pope and the English slave boys (the Angles "have the face of angels" II.1, pp. 134–35, quoted above in Chap. 1). The famous account of the conversion of King Edwin takes up chapters 9–14, including, in chapter 13, the sardonic tale of the self-seeking pagan high priest Coifi, who exclaims to the king seeking counsel about conversion: "None of your followers have devoted himself more earnestly than I have to the worship of our gods, but nevertheless there are many who receive greater benefits and greater honor from you than I do and are more successful in all their undertakings. If the gods had any power they would have helped me more readily, seeing that I have always served them with greater zeal (II.13, pp. 182–83).

This cynical speech is matched by a counselor's beautiful words on the nature of human life:

This is how the present life of man on earth, King, appears to me in comparison with that time which is unknown to us. You are sitting feasting with your ealdormen and thegns in winter time; the fire is burning on the hearth in the middle of the hall and all inside is warm, while outside the wintry storms of rain and snow are raging; and a sparrow flies swiftly through the hall. It enters in at one door and quickly flies out through the other. For the few minutes it is inside, the storm and wintry tempest cannot touch it, but after the briefest moment of calm, it flits from your sight, out of the wintry storm and into it again. So this life of man appears but for a moment; what follows or indeed what went before, we know not at all. If this new doctrine brings us more certain information, it seems right that we should accept it. (pp. 182–85)

King Edwin, "with all the nobles of his race and a vast number of the common people," received baptism (II.14, pp. 186–87). The book ends as Paulinus, who had converted Edwin and the Nor-thumbrians, retires from the north to become bishop of Rochester.

Book III treats mainly the subsequent development of the Church in Northumbria under Irish influence. But first chapter 2 narrates how King Oswald erected a large cross at Heavenfield and com-manded his army to kneel and pray before it, and then, although greatly outnumbered, advanced victoriously against Caedwalla, "the abominable leader of the Britons together with the immense force which he boasted was irresistible" (p. 215). Although Bede does not expressly call attention to the typology, the reader of Christian history cannot but note the similarity drawn between Oswald and his cross and Constantine and the vision of the cross before the battle at the Milvian bridge—an event (312) that led to the conversion of the Roman Empire to Christianity. Then chapter 3 tells how the saintly King Oswald asked the Irish elders for a bishop and received Saint Aidan from Iona to become bishop of Lindisfarne (pp. 218–19). Chapters 25 and 26, however, describe the rejection of the Iona-Lindisfarne Irish tradition when the Roman-Canterbury fac-tion, under the youthful leadership of the eloquent Wilfrid, triumphed over the Irish at the Council of Whitby, settling the question of Easter reckoning and of the type of clerical tonsure, bonding the English Church with the Continent and Rome.

The first part of book IV recounts Archbishop Theodore's apos-tolate, which was of great consequence because "he was the first of the archbishops whom the whole English Church consented to obey" (IV.2, pp. 332–33). He and his abbot Hadrian purveyed learning "in sacred and secular literature" at Canterbury, giving Latin and Greek "instruction not only in the books of holy Scripture but also in the art of meter, astronomy, and ecclesiastical computation" (pp. 332–35). Despite his advanced age, Theodore energetically organized the Church, conducted official visitations, held the important synods of Hertford (IV.5) and Hatfield (IV.15), and brought about peace between the warring kings Ecgfrith and Æthelred.

Chapter 23 (earlier version, chapter 21)[22] tells about the royal lady Hild, who became the abbess of the double monastery of men and women at Whitby. She became Archbishop Theodore's powerful confederate against the ambitious Wilfrid. In chapter 24 (22) Bede relates the precious story about her subject, the herdsman Cædmon, who was originally so intimidated by poetic recitation that he fled the hall to avoid it but became the first known Anglo-Saxon *scop*.

He had lived in the secular habit until he was well advanced in years and had never learned any songs. Hence sometimes at a feast, when for the sake of providing entertainment, it had been decided that they should all sing in turn, when he saw the harp approaching him, he would rise up in the middle of feasting, go out, and return home.

On one such occasion when he did so, he left the place of feasting and went to the cattle byre, as it was his turn to take charge of them that night. In due time he stretched himself out and went to sleep, whereupon he dreamt that someone stood by him, saluted him, and called him by name: "Caedmon," he said, "sing me something." Caedmon answered, "I cannot sing; that is why I left the feast and came here because I could not sing." Once again the speaker said, "Nevertheless you must sing to me." "What must I sing?" said Caedmon. "Sing," he said, "about the beginning of created things." Thereupon Caedmon began to sing verses which he had never heard before in praise of God the Creator, of which this is the general sense: "Now we must praise the Maker of the heavenly kingdom, the power of the Creator and his counsel, the deeds of the Father of glory and how he, since he is the eternal God, was the Author of all marvels and first created the heavens as a roof for the children of men and then, the almighty Guardian of the human race, created the earth." (pp. 415–17)

Cædmon's first little poem in Old English has been inserted in the margins of the Latin text in a number of early manuscripts of the *Historia*. Literary historians have analyzed Cædmon's verse for what it can tell us about oral composition, poetic rumination ("like some clean animal chewing the cud," pp. 418–19), and Old English versification.[23] Bede, however, only provides the Latin paraphrase with the perceptive note: "This is the sense but not the order of the words which he sang as he slept; for it is not possible to translate verse, however well composed, literally from one language to another without detriment to its beauty and dignity" (pp. 416–17). This is but a very early version of Robert Frost's remark that what is lost in translation is the poetry.

Bede devotes the last chapters of book IV.27–30 to the monk and bishop, Saint Cuthbert. As the great Theodore appears as the model of a Roman prelate, Cuthbert is the exemplar of the Irish monastic preacher in full union with Rome. For these chapters Bede depends on both the anonymous life and his own prose life of the saint.

The fifth book brings the *History* from the time of Cuthbert's successor (after 677) up to the present (mid-731), with some back-tracking to trace developments of earlier events. In chapter 20 he speaks of his admired friends Abbot Albinus, to whom he wrote the discussed letter, and Bishop Acca, to whom he dedicated most of his theological works. In chapter 23 he considers the state of the Church in the present period of smiling peace and serenity. The last sentence of the chapter incorporates Psalms 96:1 and 29:3 in a hymn of thanks, but it also includes a subtle eschatological note, because the spread and acceptance of the faith among "the multitude of isles" at the ends of the earth is seen as one of the signs of the final days (pp. 560–61). But Bede, who in his exegesis of apocalyptic texts is always careful to note that "of that day and hour no one knows" (Matt. 24:36; cf. 25:13, Rev. 3:3, and *De temporum ratione* 67.594–95), prudently says no more. His subsequent Letter to Ecgbert sounds, as we have seen in chapter 4, a more ominous but still idealistic note.

Bede completed his history some 1255 years ago. With such a temporal and cultural gulf, it should not seem odd that modern students, even while recognizing its clarity, order, literary and historical value, should be puzzled and troubled by some of its qualities. Secular events and data form our modern sense of history; Bede's was formed by the Bible, the Fathers, and the Church with its liturgy. Bede came to history as an exegete, who had learned his trade from immersion in the hermeneutics of Ambrose, Jerome, Augustine (particularly), and Gregory. He spoke that idiom.[24] His biblical Christian view holds that there is a continuous and close bond between eternity and time, that time at once creates a distance between past and present but also links the two, and that time marks the continuity of the people of God on the way to God's future. Bede's decision to begin his history of time from Christ's Incarnation is absolutely fitting, for it allows him to express not only the present state of historical development but also the linearity of time linked to the central event of Christ's birth and the relationship between events B.C. and personages of the Old Testament who prefigure, foreshadow, and explain the meaning of the New Testament. Since the Incarnation also marks the beginning of Christian salvation history, it serves as the basis for Bede's Christocentric view of history, his hope for reform, and his idealistic assurance that, despite all setbacks, God and humanity will be victorious. Bede's historical outlook is therefore at once achronological (typical, symbolic, allegorical, timeless) and temporal (continuous, distinct, unique). Such a religious historicity is strange to the reader today.

Furthermore, Bede's sense of history encompasses both human and divine causality, the ordinary working out of God's plan, human contribution to history for good and ill, and the miraculous. The recounting of the miraculous in the *Ecclesiastical History* is most likely to cause the modern reader to balk or be amused. Historians of a former generation, even great ones who convinced the academic world of Bede's eminent qualities as an historian, rejected the religious and theological elements as foreign to the writing of true history; they considered that Bede's inclusion and use of miracle stories detracted from a work that in other places manifested accuracy, attention to eyewitnesses and reliable sources, and great synthetic analysis.[25] In recent years scholars have begun to recognize and study Bede in the context of his own cultural milieu and have gained a new sympathy for the whole of his historiography.[26] Bede believed in miracles as part of his world and of his history. History and hagiography are not different categories. God could work miracles and did, though with Gregory and Augustine Bede believed that physical miracles were more frequent because more necessary in the early days of the Church, and that God worked greater miracles in people's souls than he did in palpable wonders. But he also knew of latter-day occurrences, which he used for his purposes in the *History*. Of the fifty-one accounts of miracles and the miraculous he relates, most (twenty-eight) appear in the last two books, that is, after the conversion of the Anglo-Saxons. The miracles are not demonstrations of force or magic; Bede usually calls them *signa* as in the Bible, not *miracula*, for they are indications, signs of an inner

meaning, not ascetical fireworks. They are rewards and special bless-
ings. They encourage, enrich, and confirm those who have already
received the faith. Particularly for the later miracles Bede takes care
to identify sources. Except for the wonder he experienced while
writing the life of Cuthbert, he does not record the miracles as an
eyewitness. But they form part of the ecclesiastical history of his
nation, the account of the workings of God amongst his people.

Chapter Six
Bede's Legacy

During his lifetime, Bede was primarily a teacher. He left his mark not only by his books but also by his teaching, in which he had such joy. A few of his disciples proved worthy of their master. His former pupil, Archbishop Ecgbert, attempted to put into practice Bede's counsels for improving and reforming the Church, and as a result incurred with the king a formal rebuff from the pope. Ecgbert, while remaining active as a writer, entrusted his school at York to Æthelberht; in turn, his disciple Alcuin carried Bede's scholarship to the court and school of Charlemagne. Even though loath to let Bede's works out of his sight, Alcuin allowed some of his own collection to be copied at the urgent bidding of the abbess Gisla, sister of Charlemagne.[1] Another pupil of Bede, Cuthbert (not to be confused with his namesake, Saint Cuthbert), became abbot of Wearmouth-Jarrow after Hwætberht; his letters, including the famous account of Bede's death, are of historical value.

As a teacher, Bede began writing for his students in the monastery; but soon his reputation spread through the ecclesiastical network and his writings were sought in other English centers of learning. His works passed first to other Northumbrian centers, such as Hexham and York, then farther afield to the south, London and Canterbury, then with the Anglo-Saxon missionaries to the Continent.[2] While composing and disseminating his own works, Bede served as his own secretary, copyist, and corrector (as many a great teacher after him has also had to do); under Abbot Ceolfrith the Wearmouth-Jarrow scriptorium became fully engaged in the writing and copying of the great pandects and other biblical and liturgical manuscripts, all in formal uncial script. After this need was satisfied, however, the requests from England and the Continent for Bede's works became so urgent that it seems the scriptorium had to adopt a more quickly written Anglo-Saxon miniscule script in small format, to handle the demand.[3] The exactions made on the scriptoria of both Wearmouth-Jarrow and York are clear from the pleading letters especially of the Anglo-Saxon missionaries on the Continent, such as Boniface (Winfrith) and Lul. After writing to Archbishop Ecgbert of York for copies of Bede (*EHD* I, no. 179, p. 824), in 746 Boniface, as archbishop of Mainz, also wrote to Abbot Hwætberht of Wearmouth-Jarrow: "We ask that you will deign to have copied and sent to us certain of the works of that most skillful investigator of the Scriptures, the monk Bede, who, we have heard, has lately shone in the house of God among you with knowledge of the Scriptures like a candle of the Church" (*EHD* I, no. 180, p. 825).

The scriptorium could not keep up. Even in our age of easy graphic reproduction, the poignancy of the effort still comes through in a letter from Abbot Cuthbert in 764, answering the request of Lul, who succeeded Boniface at Mainz, for some copies of Bede's writings:

Now truly, since you have asked for some of the works of the blessed father, for your love I have prepared what I could, with my pupils, according to our capacity. I have sent in accordance with your wishes the books about the man of God, Cuthbert, composed in verse and prose. And if I could have done more, I would gladly have done so. For the conditions of the past winter oppressed the island of our race very horribly with cold and ice and long and widespread storms of wind and rain, so that the hand of the scribe was hindered from producing a great number of books. (*EHD* I, no. 185, p. 832)

Besides the evidence for Bede's popularity provided in the correspondence of the time, we have indication of his continuing authority from the widespread dissemination of his works and from the number of borrowings that authors made from his works. The largest number of sermons (fifty-six) of any churchman, including the ancient Fathers, to be found in the very popular early medieval homiliary of Paul the Deacon is that of Bede.[4] Authors mined his work for inclusion in their own. Felix of Crowland used both Bede's lives of Saint Cuthbert in his *Life of St. Guthlac* (c. 749).[5] Alcuin, who constantly refers to Bede as "our teacher," incorporates material from the *Ecclesiastical History*, the lives of Saint Cuthbert, and many of the commentaries.[6] Ælfric borrowed heavily from Bede's scientific works for his *De temporibus anni*. For Amalarius of Metz, who quotes from Bede extensively, Bede's authority suffices as guarantee of truth (PL 105.1164C).

By the ninth century, the admiration for Bede was so extensive that he was enthroned among the Fathers of the Church, on a par with the four great Doctors, by churchmen as eminent as Alcuin and Claudius of Turin. The Council of Aachen (836) decreed Bede to have the same kind of authority as the earlier Fathers. In Ireland he was "Bede the great priest, the sage, a man of God's grace in wisdom and holiness," revered as a saint, *noibh*.[7]

Despite the annalistic continuations to the *Ecclesiastical History* to the year 766, real history died with Bede, not to be reborn in England until the twelfth-century historians. William of Malmesbury considered himself Bede's successor, and set about filling the chasm in literary historiography between their centuries.[8] Nonetheless, Bede's history served chroniclers for the intervening centuries. *The Anglo-Saxon Chronicle* relies mainly on Bede's *History* for all events between the Roman occupation of Britain and 731. Respect for the *History* itself and its value continued. During the reign of King Alfred (871–99), a talented Mercian translated the bulk of Bede's *Historia ecclesiastica* into Old English, omitting most of the letters, documents, and poems quoted in the original as well as material outside English affairs. It is perhaps because of this version that some today think Bede wrote the history in English. It is possible that King Alfred, eager to add to the little essential library an English history for ignorant clergy and nobility, commissioned this translation. Students of Old English usually read in Anglo-Saxon the beautiful stories of Gregory encountering the Anglian slaveboys, of King Edwin's counselor comparing the human life span to the flight of a sparrow in and out of the hall, and of Cædmon's miraculous gift of poetry and his gentle life and death.[9] Though the translator is generally careful, his grasp of Latin is not always sure (for instance, he sometimes takes the feminine ablative of the first declension for the nominative). But occasionally he turns the English phrase better than Bede's Latin one. Stanley B. Greenfield observes, "The Old English translator had something of a poetic turn of mind, exhibited in a vocabulary rich in poetic diction, in metaphoric creativity—he translates, for instance, the bald *paruissimo spatio* of the conversion-of-Edwin sparrow simile into *an eagan bryhtm* 'the twinkling of an eye'—and in a poetic sense of economy that nevertheless renders the Latin text closely and faithfully, with little extraneous matter."[10] In 991 Abbot Ælfric, no mean stylist, pays it the honor of a direct borrowing from some sections. It remains an important linguistic and literary legacy of the Anglo-Saxon world.

The tradition of translating the *Historia ecclesiastica* into English continues unabated to this day, with at least half a dozen available now.

The most impressive testimony to Bede's immediate fame and influence is the number of manuscripts of Bede's works either still extant or entered in medieval library catalogues, from the eighth century onwards. Because of the Viking depredations and subsequent barbarities in England, very few early manuscripts of Bede survived in England, but a large number did survive on the Continent. The exegetical writings come down to us, as Laistner remarks with uncharacteristic abandon, "in innumerable manuscripts."[11] Although some of Bede's other works are extant only in a few manuscripts (for instance, the *History of the Abbots* is found in only six), the *Ecclesiastical History* exists in over 150, including two from Northumbria datable to within a few years of Bede's death (see Frontispiece).[12]

One measure of the importance Bede had in the Middle Ages is the multitude of works falsely attributed to him. "For several centuries after his death," notes Laistner, "his authority as a theologian ranked next to that of the four Latin doctors and the list of works going under his name, but not by him, is long."[13] Most of the attributions were apparently not fraudulent; they resulted from anonymous works being attracted to his in manuscript collections. Many of these false pieces are contained in the editions of Giles and Migne, and the student must beware, for they are not always identified as spurious.[14]

Bede worked no miracles during his life. In *The Bishops, Kings and Saints of York* (vv. 1315–18), Alcuin records only one, done posthumously, a cure of a sick man surrounded by Bede's relics.[15] Nonetheless, Bede was instantly proclaimed a saint, and his cult spread rapidly.[16] Scholars, renowned more for diligence and assiduity than for spectacular acts, can feel gratified that this patron's sanctity was not proclaimed by loud marvels. The monasteries of Fulda and later Glastonbury displayed his relics for veneration. Perhaps the greatest tribute to their worth is the fact that in the eleventh century his bones were considered important enough to steal from Jarrow to honor Durham, which already had those of Saint Cuthbert.[17] Today Bede is still honored there in the front of the cathedral, and Cuthbert in the rear, close together but, as in life, not too close.

In his *Paradiso*, Dante, with a kind of divine irony, resolves opposing standards and personalities; for example in canto XI, verses 43–117, he has the traditionally cool and rational Thomas Aquinas of the rival Dominican order praise Saint Francis in exuberant Franciscan language. With the same kind of irony, in Canto X.181 Dante also put Bede in the company of Isidore, whom Bede in life could not approve as a scholar. Not only literature but also history offers some ironies about Bede. Bede, the hater of heresy and strenuous defender of Rome and the pope's authority against the Celts, was favored by both Catholics and Protestants in the Reformation. The Wycliffites honored him as an early translator of the Bible; the martyrologist John Foxe praised his knowledge of the Scriptures and his holiness. On the other hand, the Catholic apologist Thomas Stapleton translated Bede's *Ecclesiastical History* and dedicated it to Queen Elizabeth in the hopes of converting her by its orthodoxy. R. W. Chambers concludes, "To be simultaneously applauded by Foxe and Stapleton was a triumph, and is characteristic of Bede's wide appeal."[18] Pope Leo XIII, who denied the validity of Anglican Holy Orders, proclaimed Bede doctor of the universal Church in 1899. When Prince Charles and Lady Diana visited Pope John Paul II in 1984, they presented him with a copy of Bede's *Ecclesiastical History*. Anglican, Episcopal, and Catholic churches continue to be dedicated in his name.

What has Bede contributed to the treasury of human thought and letters? In his own day he was more esteemed as an educator and exegete; in our time, as an historian, indeed as the father of English history. Many editions and translations of his *History* exist, and he is studied and written about mostly by historians. The *History* remains the single most important source of all our knowledge of England from the coming of Saint Augustine to Kent in 597 till the book's completion in 731 or 732. It has never lacked readers since before it was completed. (See Chap. 5.) For centuries no historian would write as clearly, richly, and eruditely as he.

But this book should have made it clear that Bede's worth lies, in varying degrees, in all the fields he wrote about. Historians of education are reevaluating his contributions to the development of curricular subjects and the monastic schools. Historians of culture are examining his effect on early medieval attitudes towards grammar and rhetoric. Linguists and literary critics find his synthetic approach to language and literature suggestive, his ideas about sign and metaphor interesting precursors to modern theories. These and other topics we have seen in Chapter 2.

Although some of Bede's homilies are still used in the divine office said by priests and religious of the Catholic Church, few students of theology study his exegetical works now. Nevertheless, historians such as Gerald Bonner, Giosuè Musca, Claudio Leonardi, Paul Meyvaert, Roger Ray, Glenn Olsen, and Jan Davidse have stressed the interpenetration and interaction of exegesis and historiography in Bede's scholarship. Furthermore, because Bede had an intense commitment to literal truth and at the same time a profound sensitivity to allegorical interpetation, he has remained a model and paragon for theologians and humanists, even during the greatest modifications in taste and hermeneutic approach.[19] Other merits of his exegesis we have seen in Chapter 3.

Recent developments in the study of Insular Latin (medieval Latin in the British Isles and its influence on the Continent) have brought renewed interest to the study of the styles and techniques of Aldhelm, Bede, and Alcuin. Scholars, particularly at the universities of Cambridge, Oxford, and Toronto, have intensified their investigations in the writings of these authors and have published a number of important texts and studies. Yet, while everyone praises Bede's style, no one has as yet found its model or thoroughly analyzed its unique characteristics. Bede's various literary modes, discussed in Chapter 4, have received considerable attention lately. Hagiography, which was something of an embarrassment for serious medievalists in the past, is now stimulating a great deal of sympathetic analysis, particularly for what it tells us of social attitudes and practices. Although earlier scholars such as Bertram Colgrave produced excellent editions and studies, students now find that in Bede's hagiography they still have a wide field of sociohistory to plough.

All these aspects of Bede's writings are matters for worthwhile research. But what Bede has given as a legacy is larger than any of them. He was not a modern scholar, sharing our accumulated wisdom, views, and prejudices.[20] It would be foolish and unscholarly to treat him as one. We must expect him to share the beliefs and attitudes of his time about, for instance, miracles, the religious life, and monarchy, though we become accustomed to his treating such matters with restraint and good sense. But he was the great scholar of his age, and to understand the mentality and the ideals of that age, we turn to him. He had a unitary and unifying vision of his God, his world, his Church, his vocation, his learning, teaching, and writing. With clarity and simplicity, he conveyed that entirety, writing about everything he thought important for others to learn and to assimilate. Although he composed his works over a span of forty years in every subject of interest to his students and friends, they are all unified, concatenated by a principle of interpreting God's words and actions in history, including, essentially, the history of his English nation in that grand scheme. He wrote furiously in his mature years to accomplish this great goal. His energetic enterprise stands as a monument to the best of medieval monasticism and humanism.[21]

William Wordsworth also decided to write an ecclesiastical history of his nation, but in his own way. In order that "certain points in the Ecclesiastic History of our Country might advantageously be presented to view in Verse," Wordsworth composed *The Ecclesiastical Sonnets*. In one of them, I.23, he attempted to capture the intellectual energy and moral spirit of Bede:

> But what if One, through grove or flowery mead,
> Indulging thus at will the creeping feet
> Of a voluptuous indolence, should meet
> Thy hovering shade, O venerable Bede!
> The saint, the scholar, from a circle freed
> Of toil stupendous, in a hallowed seat,
> Of learning, where thou heard'st the billows beat
> On a wild coast, rough monitors to feed
> Perpetual industry. Sublime Recluse!
> The recreant soul, that dares to shun the debt
> Imposed on human kind, must first forget
> Thy diligence, thy unrelaxing use
> Of a long life; and, in the hour of death,
> The last dear service of the passing breath![22]

Notes and References

Frontispiece

1. This Northumbrian manuscript was written in pointed Insular script around the year 737, only two years after Bede's death. For a facsimile of this manuscript, see *The Moore Bede: Cambridge University Library MS Kk. 5. 16,* ed. Peter Hunter Blair and Roger A. B. Mynors, Early English Manuscripts in Facsimile, vol. 9 (Copenhagen: Rosenkilde & Bagger, 1959). You may wish to compare it with the approximately coeval manuscript, Leningrad Public Library MS Q. v. I. 18, *The Leningrad Bede,* ed. O. Arngart, EEMF, vol. 2 (Copenhagen: Rosenkilde & Bagger, 1952).

Preface

1. For a sample of the fame he enjoyed even in the next generation, see the Letter of Boniface to Hwætberht (746–47), *EHD* I, no. 180, p. 825; Letter of Cuthbert, abbot of Wearmouth, to Lul (764), *EHD* I, no. 185, p. 832; Alcuin, *The Bishops, Kings, and Saints of York,* ed. Peter Godman (Oxford: Clarendon Press, 1982), lines 1301–18, pp. 102–5; Letter 216, *Alcuini epistolae,* MGH, Epistolarum IV, *Epistolae Karolini Aevi,* ed. E. Duemmler (Berlin: Weidmann, 1896), 2:360. See also Chap. 6 below, and Dorothy Whitelock, *After Bede,* Jarrow Lecture 1960. For the "father of" titles given him, see the same lecture, p. 1; Dom David Knowles, Introduction to *Bede's Ecclesiastical History of the English Nation* (London: J. M. Dent, 1958), p. v; and Charles W. Jones, "Bede," in *Dictionary of the Middle Ages* (New York: Charles Scribner's Sons, 1983), 2:155, col. b. Jones also confers on him the title "Father of Carolingian Schools," in "Bede's Place in Medieval Schools," in *Famulus Christi,* ed. Gerald Bonner (London: SPCK, 1976), p. 261. Continental historians, far from accusing English historians of chauvinism, agree as a rule with the English verdict. For them Bede is also "le maître du moyen âge"— Ursmer Berlière, "L'ascèse bénédictine des origines à la fin du XIIe siècle (Paris: Desclée, 1927), p. 69. See also Giosuè Musca, *Il venerabile Beda, storico dell'alto medioevo* (Bari, Italy: Dedalo Libri, 1973), pp. 7–9.

2. See Patrick Wormald, "Bede, the *Bretwaldas* and the Origins of the *Gens Anglorum,*" in *Ideal and Reality in Frankish and Anglo-Saxon Society: Studies Presented to J. M. Wallace-Hadrill,* ed. Patrick Wormald with Donald Bullough and Roger Collins (Oxford: Basil Blackwell, 1983), pp. 99–129, esp. pp. 120–22.

3. Peter Hunter Blair's *The World of Bede* (London: Sicker & Warburg, 1970) comes closest, but it has no treatment of Bede's largest product, his exegetical works, and makes no pretense to being a complete Bedan survey. Two earlier fairly comprehensive collections of essays by various experts, *Bede: His Life, Times, and Writings: Essays in Commemoration of the Twelfth Centenary of His Death,* ed. A. Hamilton Thompson (Oxford: Clarendon Press, 1935; reprint ed. 1969) and *Famulus Christi: Essays in Commemoration of the Thirteenth Centenary of the Birth of the Venerable Bede,* ed. Gerald Bonner (London: SPCK, 1976), though excellent, are selective, now dated, and out of print.

Chapter One

1. Michael Lapidge, Introduction to Aldhelm's *Poetic Works,* trans. Michael Lapidge and James L. Rosier (Cambridge: D. S. Brewer, 1985), p. 1. For Aldhelm's life and career, see pp. 5–9. See also Lapidge's introductory remarks to Aldhelm's *Prose Works,* trans. Michael Lapidge and Michael Herren (Ipswich, England: D. S. Brewer, 1979), p. 3. It is a matter of taste whether one prefers Bede's sobriety and modesty or Aldhelm's ostentatious flamboyance, but Lapidge overstates Aldhelm's reputation with the claim that his learning surpassed "even the learning of Bede" (*Poetic Works,* p. 1). A case might be made for Aldhelm's superior knowledge of the Latin classics, but for breadth of knowledge, clarity of style, theological and historical discernment, and encyclopedic knowledge, and much else, history has rightly accorded the palm to Bede. By the ninth century Bede was already honored as a doctor of the church and his reputation on the Continent far exceeded Aldhelm's, as historical record and the number of Bede's works in manuscripts testify. Already in the Middle Ages Aldhelm was forgotten even in England, and "he has been virtually ignored by modern scholarship" (Lapidge, Aldhelm's *Prose Works,* p. 3). Bede accords him only a short paragraph in *HE* V.18, pp. 514–15, which is laudatory of Aldhelm but gives the impression of damning with faint praise: "He had a polished (*sermone nitidus* = flashy?) style and . . . was remarkable for his erudition." Bede was charitable and discreet, so his usual method of criticizing an author (e.g., Isidore of Seville), is to say as little about him as possible, except to correct that author's specific error.

2. On Alcuin and his cultural role, see the introduction and bibliographical notes by Peter Godman to his edition of Alcuin, *The Bishops, Kings, and Saints of York,* pp. xxxiii–xciii.

3. See the preface to King Alfred's translation of Gregory the Great's *Pastoral Care,* trans. Dorothy Whitelock (with bibliographic references to the Old English), *EHD* I, no. 226, pp. 888–90. The letter indicates, and

other evidence confirms, that the waning of learning in Anglo-Saxon England occurred before the Viking depredations became endemic. See Helmut Gneuss, "King Alfred and the History of Anglo-Saxon Libraries," in *Modes of Interpretation in Old English Literature: Essays in Honour of Stanley B. Greenfield,* ed. Phyllis R. Brown, Georgia Ronan Crampton, and Fred C. Robinson (Toronto: Toronto University Press, 1986), pp. 29–49. But see also Jennifer Morrish, "King Alfred's Letter as a Source on Learning in England," in *Studies in Earlier Old English Prose,* ed. Paul E. Szarmach (Albany: State University of New York Press, 1986), pp. 87–108. Although Gneuss and Morrish agree that the decline of learning in ninth-century England preceded and was not the direct result of the Viking invasions, Morrish, using much the same data as Gneuss, argues (as do David Dumville and others) that King Alfred exaggerates the extent of the decline. Gneuss (allied with Michael Lapidge and others) gives suasive reasons for the basic truth of Alfred's assertions.

    4. For the tenth-century reform, see George Hardin Brown, "The Anglo-Saxon Monastic Revival," in *Renaissances before the Renaissance,* ed. Warren Treadgold (Stanford: Stanford University Press, 1984), pp. 99–113, and bibliography, pp. 217–18.

    5. As Sir Frank Stenton expressed it in his still magisterial *Anglo-Saxon England,* 3d ed. (Oxford: Clarendon Press, 1971), p. 177:

In the middle of the seventh century there was nothing to suggest the imminence of a great English achievement in learning and literature. The strongest of English kings was an obdurate heathen. The country was distracted by wars which destroyed the peace of scholars, and offered little but a succession of well-worn themes to the makers of heroic verse. The Christian faith, which was to carry imagination into new worlds, was only secure in the extreme south east of the island. Within a hundred years England had become the home of a Christian culture which influenced the whole development of letters and learning in western Europe. The greatest historical work of the early Middle Ages had been written in a northern monastery, and English poets had begun to give a permanent form to heroic traditions. There is nothing in European history closely parallel to this sudden development of a civilization by one of the most primitive peoples established within the ancient Roman empire.

    6. See Joel T. Rosenthal, "Bede's Ecclesiastical History and the Material Condition of Anglo-Saxon Life," *Journal of British Studies* 19 (1979):1–17, esp. 15–16. For socioeconomic information about the period, all authorities, such as Stenton, Hill, and Rosenthal, depend on data furnished by Bede in *HE.*

    7. The phrase is applied to ecclesiastical documents by David Hill

in *An Atlas of Anglo-Saxon England* (Toronto: University of Toronto Press, 1981), p. 23.

8. See Wormald, "Bede, the *Bretwaldas* and the Origins of the *Gens Anglorum*," pp. 99–129.

9. See Peter Hunter Blair, *Northumbria in the Days of Bede* (New York: St. Martin's Press, 1976), esp. pp. 39–49; R. I. Page, *Life in Anglo-Saxon England* (London: B. T. Batsford, 1970), pp. 1–12. For kings who abdicated to adopt the religious life, see Clare Stancliffe, "Kings Who Opted Out," in *Ideal and Reality*, ed. Wormald, pp. 154–76.

10. Stenton, *Anglo-Saxon England*, pp. 87–95; Hill, *Atlas of Anglo-Saxon England*, p. 31.

11. On the Welshman Gildas and his *De excidio Brittaniae*, written around 540, from which Bede draws much of his information for *HE* I.1–22, see Gildas, *The Ruin of Britain, and Other Works*, ed. and trans. Michael Winterbottom (Totowa, N.J.: Rowman & Littlefield, 1978); and *Gildas: New Approaches*, ed. Michael Lapidge (Woodbridge, Suffolk, England: Boydell Press, 1984).

12. As a confirmation that the tradition of Gregory's fondness for punning on the name Angli was not fabricated by the English writers, we have the pope's letter of July 598 to Eulogius, bishop of Alexandria, in which he rejoices in the conversion of the "gens *Anglorum* in mundi *angulo* posita" ("the English located in the corner of the world"; italics mine). Cited in Michael Richter, "Bede's *Angli:* Angles or English?" *Peritia* 3 (1984): 104. On Bede's admiration and emulation of Gregory, see Paul Meyvaert, *Bede and Gregory the Great*, Jarrow Lecture 1964, reprinted in *Benedict, Gregory, Bede and Others* (London: Variorum Reprints, 1977).

13. Henry Mayr-Harting, *The Coming of Christianity to England* (New York: Schocken Books, 1972), p. 62.

14. On the religious and doctrinal importance of the paschal controversy between the Irish and Roman parties, see J. Campbell, "Bede," in *Latin Historians*, ed. T. A. Dorey (London: Routledge & Kegan Paul, 1966), pp. 180–81; Stenton, *Anglo-Saxon England*, pp. 122–27. For an introduction into the complexities of paschal dates, see Charles W. Jones, *Bedae opera de temporibus* (Cambridge, Mass.: Mediaeval Academy of America, 1943), pp. 6–104.

15. On the development of the medieval cloister, see the papers from the Cloister Symposium, 1972, in *Gesta* 12 (1973), esp. Walter Horn, "On the Origins of the Medieval Cloister," 13–52, and Paul Meyvaert, "The Medieval Monastic Claustrum," 53–59.

16. Most of the information we have about Wearmouth-Jarrow, its great library, and its abbots comes to us from the *Life of Ceolfrith* (possibly by Bede), Bede's *History of the Abbots of Wearmouth-Jarrow* (both discussed in Chap. 5 below), Bede's sermon on Benedict Biscop (CCSL 122, pp.

88–94, discussed in Chap. 4) and Bede's entries in *HE*, e.g., IV.18; V.21. For some modern assessments, see Eric Fletcher, *Benedict Biscop,* Jarrow Lecture 1981; Patrick Wormald, "Bede and Benedict Biscop," in *Famulus Christi,* ed. Bonner, pp. 141–69; Peter Hunter Blair, *The World of Bede,* pp. 175–94; Judith McClure, "Bede and the Life of Ceolfrid," *Peritia* 3 (1984): 71–84.

17. For the vicissitudinous life of Wilfrid, see his biography by Eddius Stephanus, ed. Bertram Colgrave (Cambridge: Cambridge University Press, 1927); Henry Mayr-Harting, *The Coming of Christianity to England,* pp. 129–47; D. P. Kirby, "Northumbria in the Time of Wilfrid," and D. H. Farmer, "Saint Wilfrid," in *Saint Wilfrid at Hexham,* ed. D. P. Kirby (Newcastle, England: Oriel Press, 1974), pp. 1–60.

18. Wilfrid also employed Continental models and masters for the renovation of the cathedral at York, the construction of the basilican church of dressed stone at Ripon, and of the church at Hexham, the like of which, men claimed, was not to be seen beyond the Alps.

19. See Paul Meyvaert, "Bede and the Church Paintings at Wearmouth-Jarrow," *Anglo-Saxon England* 8 (1979):63–77.

20. Bede, *HA* 7, p.376, says "about seventeen" monks began the new establishment; the anonymous *History* 11, trans. Boutflower, p. 62, says twenty-two. This discrepancy may result from an early copyist's easy confusion of roman numerals XVII and XXII.

21. See Dom David Knowles, *The Monastic Order in England,* 2d ed. (Cambridge: Cambridge University Press, 1963), pp. 21–23; Patrick Wormald, "Bede and Benedict Biscop," in *Famulus Christi,* ed. Bonner, pp. 141–46. The tenth-century English monastic reform prescribed the Rule of Benedict as the norm.

22. On the nature and history of the Benedictine rule, see *RB: The Rule of St. Benedict,* ed. Timothy Fry (Collegeville, Minn.: Liturgical Press, 1981), pp. 3–155, and the selected bibliography, pp. xxxii–vi. See also David Knowles, *Christian Monasticism* (New York: McGraw-Hill, 1969), and C. H. Lawrence, *Medieval Monasticism* (London and New York: Longman, 1984).

23. P. Wormald, "Bede and Benedict Biscop," p. 144.

24. See Wormald, p. 143 and n. 15; Henry Mayr-Harting, *The Venerable Bede, the Rule of St. Benedict, and Social Class,* Jarrow Lecture 1976; Hugh Farmer, "The Studies of Anglo-Saxon Monks (A.D. 600–800)," in *Los monjes y los estudios* (Poblet, Spain: Abadia de Poblet, 1963), pp. 87–88; *HE,* ed. Colgrave and Mynors, pp. xxiii–xxv. It is not surprising that earlier historians of monasticism assumed that Benedict Biscop and his monks, particularly Bede, not only epitomized Benedictine piety but were indeed true followers of the Benedictine rule. See the Count de Montalembert, *The Monks of the West, from St. Benedict to St. Bernard*

(London: John Nimmo, 1896), 4:179: Benedict Biscop "took care to constitute his community upon the immovable basis of the rule of St. Benedict"; see also 239–71 for Bede.

25. See the plate in *The Anglo-Saxons,* ed. J. Campbell (Ithaca, N. Y.: Cornell University Press, 1982), p. 74; Rosemary Cramp, "Monkwearmouth and Jarrow: The Archaeological Evidence," in *Famulus Christi,* ed. Bonner, pp. 5–18; Horn, "On the Origins of the Medieval Cloister," 13–52, esp. 38–39.

26. Bede says "about 600," *HA* 17, p. 388; *Life of Ceolfrith,* chap. 33, p. 81, says "more than 600."

27. For investigations of the Codex Amiatinus, see R. L. S. Bruce-Mitford, *The Art of the Codex Amiatinus,* Jarrow Lecture 1967; Bonifatius Fischer, "Bibelausgaben des frühen Mittelalters," *La Bibbia nell'alto medioevo,* Settimane di studio del centro italiano de studi sull'alto medioevo, no. 10 (Spoleto, Italy: Presso la sede del centro, 1963), esp. 560–61, and "Codex Amiatinus und Cassiodor," *Biblische Zeitschrift,* 6 (1962):57–79.

28. Malcolm Parkes, *The Scriptorium of Wearmouth-Jarrow,* Jarrow Lecture 1982.

29. See Mayr-Harting, *The Venerable Bede,* pp. 10–12.

30. Only three other men by the name Bæda appear in early records, a monk, a priest at Lindisfarne, and a chieftain of the Lindisfari. See Plummer I, p. lxxviii, n. and II, index nominum, s.v.

31. Mayr-Harting, *The Venerable Bede,* pp. 16–17. Alcuin says of Bede that "with loving concern his parents [*cura parentum*] had made him enter at the age of seven the cloistered precincts of the monastery of Jarrow" (*The Bishops, Kings, and Saints of York,* ed. Godman, pp. 102–3, ll. 1294–95); Bede himself speaks more vaguely of *cura propinquorum.* This appears to be a deliberate suppression of familial information.

32. *RB: The Rule of St. Benedict,* ed. Fry, prologue 50 (pp. 166–67), 4.78, 58.9, 60.9, 61.5.

33. On child-oblates, see Knowles, *Monastic Order in England,* pp. 417–18. Sr. M. Thomas Aquinas Carroll, *The Venerable Bede: His Spiritual Teachings* (Washington, D.C.: Catholic Universtiy of America Press, 1946), pp. 2–3, asserts that ecclesiastical regulations prohibited any other than a parent from offering the son as an oblate. Whether Bede was entered as an oblate (that is, offered by his relatives to God as a monk) or as a pupil to be trained in letters, who then chose to remain as a monk, we do not know for certain; but he remained contentedly for life "in the school of the service of the Lord." (*RB: The Rule of St. Benedict,* prologue 45, pp. 164–65). We know of some few laymen educated as externs in monastic schools; see Knowles, *Monastic Order,* pp. 488–89.

34. For the meaning of *antiphon* in the rule, see *RB: The Rule of St. Benedict,* ed. Fry, pp. 401–3.

35. See Plummer I, pp. xii and 374; Dorothy Whitelock, "Bede and His Teachers and Friends," in *Famulus Christi,* ed. Bonner, pp. 21–22.

36. Alcuin, Letter 284, in MGH, Epistolarum IV, *Epistolae Karolini Aevi,* ed. Duemmler, 2:443; see letter 217, p. 360, for Alcuin's attitude towards Bede and his work. Concerning Bede's spirituality, see Carroll's *Venerable Bede,* pp. 1–66.

37. Further, see Plummer II, p.360; Whitelock, "Bede and His Teachers and Friends," p. 23; George Henderson, *Bede and the Visual Arts,* Jarrow Lecture 1980.

38. Roger Ray, in a long-delayed essay on Bede to appear in *Aufstieg und Niedergang der römischen Welt.* He adds: "Certainly his monastic schooling did not make him a Christian humanist. There is no evidence that Bede undertook an independent study of what in the Carolingian schools would be called the *trivium* and *quadrivium.* For him the liberal arts were exegetical and pedagogical resources, not autonomous disciplines."

39. "It seems probable that Bede was a 'choirmaster' *(cotidianam cantandi in ecclesia curam)* in much the same sense as Eddius Stephanus, Hucbald of St-Amand, and Notker Balbulus," says Charles W. Jones in his introduction to Bede's *Opera didascalia* (CCSL 123A, p. viii).

40. M. L. W. Laistner, *Thought and Letters in Western Europe,* A.D. *500 to 900,* 2d ed. (Ithaca, N.Y.: Cornell University Press, 1966), p. 16. See also Paul Meyvaert, "Bede the Scholar," in *Famulus Christi,* ed. Bonner, pp. 47–51.

41. For Bede's "mystic-monastic" reading and interpretation of Scripture, see Claudio Leonardi, "Il venerabile Beda e la cultura des secolo VIII," in *I problemi dell'occidente nel secolo VIII,* Settimane di studio del centro italiano di studi sull'alto medioevo, no. 20 (Spoleto, Italy: Presso la sede del centro, 1973), 2:603–58; and Glenn W. Olsen, "From Bede to the Anglo-Saxon Presence in the Carolingian Empire," in *Angli e Sassoni al di qua e al di là del mare nell'alto medioevo,* Settimane di studio del centro italiano di studi sull'alto medioevo, no. 32 (Spoleto, Italy: Presso la sede del centro, 1986), forthcoming. I am grateful to Professor Olsen for letting me read an advance copy of this excellent article.

42. M. L. W. Laistner, "The Library of the Venerable Bede," in *Bede, His Life, Times, and Writings,* ed. Thompson, pp. 237–66. Many scholars, from H. Quentin on, have discovered numerous sources not listed in Laistner's scholarly but incomplete work. Paul Meyvaert and Roger Ray propose to publish an updated version of Laistner's catalogue.

43. The five-line poem, called Bede's Death Song, has often been attributed to Bede, both in the Middle Ages and in our era, but Cuthbert's statement, "in nostra quoque lingua, ut erat doctus in nostris carminibus, dicens de terribili exitu animarum e corpore" ("as he was learned in our poems, he also was speaking in our tongue about the fearful passage of

souls from the body"), does not say the poem was his, only that he knew it, as others. Colgrave, in a note on *HE,* ed. Colgrave and Mynors, pp. 580–81, declares: "Only a comparatively small group of the MSS. of the Letter attribute the composition of the poem to Bede himself, and those the later ones. So the evidence for Bede's authorship is by no means strong." For the manuscript history of the letter and the song, see Elliott van Kirk Dobbie, *The Manuscripts of Cædmon's Hymn and Bede's Death Song, with a Critical Text of the Epistola Cuthberti de obitu Bedae* (New York: Columbia University Press, 1937), with further information about another manuscript by Neil R. Ker in *Medium Aevum* 8 (1939):40–44. The authenticity of the letter was called in question by Whitney F. Bolton, "Epistola Cuthberti De Obitu Bedae: A Caveat," *Medievalia et Humanistica* 1 (1970):127–39, but the charge has been met with either silence or incredulity.

44. The clauses, "facere studuit . . . et de libris Rotarum Ysidori episcopi exceptiones quasdam, dicens 'Nolo ut pueri mei mendacium legant, et in hoc post meum obitum sine fructu laborent,' " are capable of two meanings depending on the interpretation of *exceptiones,* both possible in the Latin of the time, and a number of scholars have taken sides on the issue. If it means "excerpts," then Bede was making or editing selections from Isidore; if it means "exceptions, reservations," then it means Bede was correcting Isidore's mistakes. Since Bede had criticized Isidore's scholarship before, and mentions that famous encyclopedist by name only three times, and always to refute him, I feel reasonably sure that the second meaning was intended. See Laistner, "Library of Venerable Bede," p. 256; Jones, *Bedae opera de temporibus,* pp. 131–32; and esp. Meyvaert, "Bede the Scholar," pp. 58–60.

45. M. L. Cameron, "The Sources of Medical Knowledge in Anglo-Saxon England," *Anglo-Saxon England* 11 (1983):146–47, explains the significance of Bede's gifts: "Bede, shortly before his death, shared out his few possessions among the priests of his monastery and these included linen, pepper and incense. In medieval medicine linen was used for bandages and pepper and incense were both common ingredients of potions, so that, even before Cyneheard wrote to Lull, some important foreign ingredients of the medival pharmacopœia were in the hands of a poor priest in distant Northumbria." Bede's works furnish Cameron (pp. 145–47) with evidence for the presence of late antique medical writings in Anglo-Saxon England.

Chapter Two

1. On the cultural debt owed by the Fathers, especially Jerome, to the classics, see Harald Hagendahl, *Latin Fathers and the Classics,* Göteborgs Universitets Årsskrift, vol. 64, no. 2 (Göteborg, Sweden: Elanders, 1958).

2. On the history of traditional classical education in antiquity and the early Middle Ages, see M. Roger, *L'enseignement des lettres classiques d'Ausone à Alcuin* (Paris: Picard, 1905), chaps. 1 and 4.1; H. I. Marrou, *A History of Education in Antiquity,* trans. George Lamb (Madison: University of Wisconsin Press, 1982), pt. 3; Stanley F. Bonner, *Education in Ancient Rome* (Berkeley: University of California Press, 1977), esp. pt. 3; Pierre Riché, *Education and Culture in the Barbarian West, Sixth through Eighth Centuries,* trans. John J. Contreni (Columbia: University of South Carolina Press, 1976), introduction and pt. 1. For the development of grammar from ancient to medieval times, see R. H. Robins, *Ancient and Medieval Grammatical Theory in Europe* (London: G. Bell & Sons, 1951). Martin Irvine's 1982 Harvard dissertation, "Grasping the Word: 'Ars Grammatica' and Literary Theory from Late Antiquity to the Carolingian Period" is being revised and expanded into a comprehensive study on the relationship between grammar and literary criticism in the early Middle Ages.

3. For an excellent summary of the complex history of Latin grammars on which this section is based, see Vivien Law, *The Insular Latin Grammarians* (Woodbridge, Suffolk, England: Boydell Press, 1982), chap. 2. For Donatus, see Louis Holtz, *Donat et la tradition de l'enseignement grammatical* (Paris: CNRS, 1981). The Latin grammars are to be found in *Grammatici latini,* ed. Heinrich Keil, 7 vols. and suppl. (Leipzig: Teubner, 1857–70).

4. Jerome, *Select Letters,* trans. F. A. Wright, Loeb Classical Library (London: William Heinemann; New York: G. P. Putnam's Sons, 1933), Letter 22.30, p. 127. For a study of Jerome's training and career, see J. N. D. Kelly, *Jerome, His Life, Writings, and Controversies* (London: Duckworth, 1975), and David S. Wiesen, *St. Jerome as a Satirist: A Study of Christian Thought and Letters* (Ithaca, N. Y.: Cornell University Press, 1964).

5. Augustine, *Confessions,* trans. R. S. Pine-Coffin (Harmondsworth, England, and Baltimore: Penguin, 1961), I.13, p. 33. For studies of Augustine's life, training, and career in its cultural milieu see Peter Brown, *Augustine of Hippo* (Berkeley: University of California Press, 1967); Henri-Irénée Marrou, *Saint Augustin et la fin de la culture antique* (Paris: Éditions E. de Boccard, 1958).

6. Gregory, *Epistolae* V.53a, in MGH, *Gregorii I Papae registrum epistolarum* I, p.357. For Gregory's training and career see F. Holmes Dudden, *Gregory the Great: His Place in History and in Thought,* 2 vols. (London and New York: Longmans, Green, & Co., 1905), and, more recently, Jeffrey Richards, *Consul of God: The Life and Times of Gregory the Great* (London and Boston: Routledge & Kegan Paul, 1980), esp. pp. 5–68.

7. Ambrose, *Expositio evangelii secundum Lucam* II.42 (PL 15. 1568). For Ambrose's life and career see Angelo Paredi, *St. Ambrose, His Life and Times* (Notre Dame, Ind.: University of Notre Dame Press, 1964).

8. Gregory, *Epistolae* XI.34, in MGH, *Registrum epistolarum* II.2, p. 303.

9. Jerome, Letter 70.2.

10. Augustine, *On Christian Doctrine*, trans. D. W. Robertson, Jr. (Indianapolis and New York: Bobbs-Merrill, 1958), II.28, p. 63; II.40, p. 75.

11. Gregory, *In librum primum Regum expositionum libri sex*, V.30 in PL 79.355.

12. See the classic work by Jean Leclercq, *The Love of Learning and the Desire for God* (New York: Fordham University Press, 1961).

13. *The Life of Ceolfrith*, chap. 12, trans. Boutflower, p.64, reports that Benedict Biscop "in consideration of his native wisdom and the ripeness of his counsels was wont to be somewhat frequently summoned to the royal presence." It is remarkable that Bede in *HA* does not mention Benedict's secular service, most likely passing over in silence once again that which he disapproves.

14. The rhetorical origin of these subjects is betrayed not only by textual history but also by occasional nods to speech performance, such as the remark that the device irony cannot be detected except by heaviness of pronunciation. See Donatus, *Ars grammatica* IV.6, *Grammatici latini*, ed. Keil, 4:402; repeated by Bede in *De tropis*, CCSL 118A, p. 162.

15. See Laistner, "Library of Venerable Bede," pp. 241–42, 263–66. For the meaning of grammar and its position in Bede's pedagogy, see Martin Irvine, "Bede the Grammarian and the Scope of Grammatical Studies in Eighth-Century Northumbria," *Anglo-Saxon England* 15(1986): 15–44.

16. Bede, *In Proverbia Salomonis* I.7.16 (CCSL 119B, p.58).

17. Bede, *In I Samuhelem* IV.31.1 (CCSL 119, p. 267). (The "certain one" is Tertullian, but since he himself became a heretic it would not have been decorous to give his name.)

18. Bede, *In Ezram et Neemiam libri III* I, ll. 1783–94 (CCSL 119A, pp. 285–86).

19. Bede, *In I Samuhelem* II.13.20 (CCSL 119, p.112).

20. Bede, *De arte metrica* I.24 (CCSL 123A, p.138).

21. Bede, *In I Samuhelem* II.14.28–29 (CCSL 119, p. 121). For a discussion of Bede's knowledge and use of the classics, see Plummer I, pp. l–liii, and Laistner, "Bede as a Classical and Patristic Scholar" and "The Library of the Venerable Bede," in *The Intellectual Heritage of the Early Middle Ages* (Ithaca, N.Y.: Cornell University Press, 1957), pp. 93–116 and 117–49.

22. I am indebted to Roger Ray for pointing out the true meaning and importance of this text, which Riché had misinterpreted in *Education,* p. 389. Ray contends that the rhetorical sophistication in Bede's *HE* and Letter to Plegwin as well as in the commentary on Acts 7:16 indicate Bede's knowledge of Cicero's *De inventione* or Victorinus's commentary on it, or both. Roger Ray, "Bede the Rhetorician," forthcoming in *Anglo-Saxon England* 16 (1987).

23. Other grammarians of the eighth century noted the same lack. "First let us ask why Donatus the grammarian did not write in his *artes* on the length of meter as others did?" asks the interlocutor in manuscript B.N. lat. 13025, copied at Corbie. I owe this reference to David Ganz.

24. See Robert B. Palmer's sensitive analysis of "Bede as Textbook Writer: A Study of His *De Arte Metrica,*" *Speculum* 34 (1959):573–84; also Holtz, *Donat,* p. 349.

25. See Lia Coronati, "La dottrina del tetrametro trocaico in Beda," *Romanobarbarica* 6 (1981–82):53–62.

26. Karl Halm edited the *De schematibus et tropis* in *Rhetores latini minores* (Leipzig: Teubner, 1863), pp. 607–18; Gussie Hecht Tanenhaus, in her translation of the treatise in the *Quarterly Journal of Speech* 48 (1962):237–53, names it "the first British work on rhetoric," a misnomer continued by Joseph M. Miller et al., eds., in their reprint of the translation (under the spelling Tannenhaus) in *Readings in Medieval Rhetoric* (Bloomington: Indiana University Press, 1973), pp.96–124. Historians of education and grammar have recognized the tract as grammatical, as does James J. Murphy in *Rhetoric in the Middle Ages* (Berkeley: University of California Press, 1974), pp. 76–80, but Calvin Kendall, who is the editor of the treatise in CCSL 123A, calls it "Bede's own rhetoric" in his article on "Bede's *Historia ecclesiastica:* The Rhetoric of Faith," in *Medieval Eloquence: Studies in the Theory and Practice of Medieval Rhetoric,* ed. James J. Murphy (Berkeley: University of California Press, 1978), p. 150.

27. See Ulrich Schindel, "Die Quellen von Bedas Figurenlehre," *Classica et Mediaevalia* 29 (1968):169, n. 1.

28. See Antonio Isola, "Il *De schematibus et tropis* di Beda in rapporto al *De doctrina christiana* di Agostino," *Romanobarbarica* 1 (1976):71–82.

29. See Armand Strubel, " 'Allegoria in factis' et 'Allegoria in verbis,' " *Poétique* 23 (1975):351–53.

30. For an explanation of these various exegetical modes, see Harry Caplan, "The Four Senses of Scriptural Interpretation and the Medieval Theory of Preaching," *Speculum* 4 (1929):282–90; for a more extensive history of the development of Christian allegorical interpretation, see Henri de Lubac, *Exégèse médiévale: les quatre sens de l'Écriture,* 2 vols. in 4 (Paris: Aubier, 1959–64), and Jean Daniélou, *From Shadows to Reality: Studies in Biblical Typology,* trans. W. Hibberd (London: Darton, Longman, & Todd,

1973). An excellent analysis of Gregory the Great's allegorical procedure is by Dietram Hofmann, *Die geistige Auslegung der Schrift bei Gregor dem Großen,* Münsterschwarzacher Studien, no. 6 (Münsterschwarzach, Germany: Vier-Turme-Verlag, 1968). With recent literary critical interest in symbolism and hermeneutics, Bede's exploration of allegorical interpretation has excited renewed attention. See, for instance, the articles in *Poétique* 23 (1975), esp. Strubel, " 'Allegoria in factis' et 'Allegoria in verbis'," 342–57; also valuable as a modern linguistic analysis of factual and verbal allegory is Tzvetan Todorov's "On Linguistic Symbolism," *New Literary History* 6 (1974 75):111–34.

31. Tanenhaus, "Bede's *De schematibus et tropis*—A Translation," p.252, by following Halm's reading in *Rhetores latini minores,* p. 618, with an intrusive *non* in the main clause of this sentence, translates this so that Bede's sentence is given a completely opposite meaning.

32. C. W. Jones, in the preface to CCSL 123A, p. x, is representative of the older opinion that contends the *De orthographia* represents "a teacher's notebook accumulated at random," though it was he who first suggested the analogy to Fowler's *Usage.* Anna Carlotta Dionisotti, in her carefully detailed and perceptive article, "On Bede, Grammars, and Greek," *Revue Benedictine* 92 (1982):111–41, has totally displaced the older view.

33. See M. L. W. Laistner's elaborate argument in *A Hand-List of Bede Manuscripts,* by Laistner with H. H. King (Ithaca, N.Y.: Cornell University Press, 1943), pp. 131–32; and Kendall, p. 74, and Jones, p. x, n. 6, for contrary opinions in the same volume, CCSL 123A. Although Remigius glosses *conleuita* as *diaconus* in this passage (p. 141), medieval Latin dictionaries indicate the term was frequently not so specific.

34. On Bede's use of natural science, see Jones, *Bedae opera de temporibus,* pp. 125–29; also the same author's succinct entry on Bede in the *Dictionary of Scientific Biography* (New York: Charles Scribner's Sons, 1970), 1:564–66, as well as his remarks as editor of the *Opera didascalia* in CCSL 123A, pp. xi–xii, 175, and 186. Peter Kitson, "Lapidary Traditions in Anglo-Saxon England: Part II, Bede's *Explanatio Apocalypsis* and Related Works," *Anglo-Saxon England* 12 (1983), p. 88, demonstrates from Bede's use of information in chapter 38 of Pliny's *Natural History* that contrary to Jones's opinion Bede also knew the second half of that work.

35. See CCSL 123A, p. 187, for a distribution chart of source-marks in selected manuscripts, and Charles W. Jones, "Manuscripts of Bede's *De Natura Rerum,*" *Isis* 27 (1937):430–40.

36. For specific details, see Thomas R. Eckenrode, "Venerable Bede as a Scientist," *American Benedictine Review* 22 (1971):486–507; "Venerable Bede's Theory of Ocean Tides," *American Benedictine Review* 25 (1974):56–74; and "The Growth of a Scientific Mind: Bede's Early and Late Scientific Writings," *Downside Review* 316 (1976):197–212.

37. Jones, CCSL 123A, p. 174; Laistner, *Hand-List*, p. 139.
38. On the development of the Latin ecclesiastical calendar, see Jones, *Bedae opera de temporibus*, pp. 3–122. For Bede as a chronologer and chronicler, see Wilhelm Levison, "Bede as Historian," in *Bede, His Life, Times, and Writings*, ed. Thompson, pp. 112–23.
39. On the meaning of the term *computus* see *Bedae opera de temporibus*, ed. Jones, pp.75–77. For much elucidation on Bede's works on time scholars owe a great debt to Jones's editing, as found in this volume and CCSL 123 A, B, and C, and interpretation as, for example, in chaps. 2 and 3 of *Saints' Lives and Chronicles in Early England* (Ithaca, N.Y.: Cornell University Press, 1947), pp. 16–50; and the articles: "An Early Medieval Licensing Examination," *History of Education Quarterly* 3 (1963):19–29; "Bede's Place in Medieval Schools," in *Famulus Christi*, ed. Bonner, pp.261–85. For Bede's indebtedness to a computus compiled in southern Ireland ca. 658, see Dáibhi Ó Croínín, "The Irish Provenance of Bede's Computus," *Peritia* 2 (1983):229–47.
40. See *Bedae opera de temporibus*, ed. Jones, pp. 350–51; and esp. Stenton, *Anglo-Saxon England*, pp. 97–98.

Chapter Three

1. Quite useful but limited investigations are: P. Capelle, "le rôle théologique de Bède le Vénérable," *Studia Anselmiana* 6 (1936):1–40; Claude Jenkins, "Bede as Exegete and Theologian," in *Bede: His Life, Times, and Writings*, ed. Thompson, pp. 152–200; Ansgar Willmes, "Bedas Bibelauslegung," *Archiv für Kulturgeschichte* 44 (1963):281–314; Gerald Bonner, *Saint Bede in the Western Tradition of Apocalyptic Commentary*, Jarrow Lecture 1966; Charles W. Jones, "Some Introductory Remarks on Bede's Commentary on Genesis," *Sacris Erudiri* 19 (1969–70):115–98; Meyvaert, "Bede the Scholar," pp. 40–69; and Roger Ray, "What Do We Know about Bede's Commentaries?" *Recherches de théologie ancienne et médiévale* 49 (1982):5–20.
2. See Laistner, *Hand-List*, pp. 37–38. Among the "Lost and Doubtful Works," pp. 154 ff., Laistner lists a *Liber Bedae in titulis psalmorum*, ascribed to Bede in some early manuscripts. Bonifatius Fischer, "Bedae de titulis psalmorum liber," in *Festschrift Bernhard Bischoff*, ed. Johanne Autenrieth and Franz Brunhölzl (Stuttgart, Germany: Anton Hiersemann, 1971), pp. 90–110, believes it possible from the early manuscript attributions to Bede that the text that appears in PL 93.483–1098 may be his work.
3. So Bede explains it in the prologue to *In I Samuhelem*, CCSL 119, p. 212, ll. 15–16.
4. Despite the extent and importance of Augustine's exegetical works,

and despite the numerous studies devoted to his theology and his use of particular sources, there is no synthesis and summary of his hermeneutics that I can recommend. Of some help, though dated, is Maurice Pontet, *L'exégèse de s. Augustin, prédicateur* (Paris: Aubier, 1946). For Gregory the Great's exegesis, see Hofmann, *Die geistige Auslegung*.

5. For a survey of the literature on the allegorical method of biblical commentary see n. 25, Chap. 2 above; also Beryl Smalley, *The Study of the Bible in the Middle Ages,* 2d ed. (Oxford: Basil Blackwell, 1952), chap. 1, and especially the excellent synthesis by Jones in "Bede's Commentary on Genesis," pp. 131–60.

6. See also Bede, *In Genesim* III.14.15, CCSL 118A, p. 188, ll. 1611–14; *De Templo* I, CCSL 119A, p. 148, 54–60; *In I Samuhelem,* prologus, CCSL 119, pp. 9–10, ll. 1–6 and 36–46; *Retractatio* X.5–6, CCSL 121, pp. 139–40, 1–2. See further in Plummer I, pp. lvi–lix.

7. See M. L. W. Laistner, "Antiochene Exegesis in Western Europe during the Middle Ages," *Harvard Theological Review* 40 (1947):19–31.

8. See Bernhard Bischoff, "Turning-Points in the History of Latin Exegesis in the Early Irish Church: A.D. 650–800," in *Biblical Studies: The Medieval Irish Contribution,* Proceedings of the Irish Biblical Association, no. 1 (Dublin: Dominican Publications, 1976), pp. 74–164, esp. pp. 74–75.

9. See Meyvaert, *Bede and Gregory the Great,* pp. 15–19.

10. See Augustine, *On Christian Doctrine* III.27; *De Genesi ad litteram* I.21; de Lubac, *Exégèse,* 1:643–56; Plummer I, pp. lvii–lxii; Jones, "Bede's Commentary on Genesis," pp. 138–40. My own analysis of Bede's allegorical methodology coincides with those of Plummer and especially Jones, against Spicq and Willmes, cited in Jones, p. 135.

11. "Or c'est lui qui a frappé la formule définitive du quadruple sens" ("Bede was the one who struck the definitive formula of the fourfold sense"), de Lubac, *Exégèse,* 1:664.

12. Jones in "Bede's Commentary on Genesis," pp. 142–45, provides a generally good translation of the passage from *De tropis,* but not a very satisfying discussion of it.

13. See Jones's section on Bede's critical vocabulary in "Bede's Commentary on Genesis," pp. 151–66.

14. For a list of some of the standard symbolic words, see Plummer I, p. lix, n. 8.

15. For a brief catalogue of this apparently arbitrary and subjective process in Bede, see Plummer I, pp. lix–lxi. For a translation of parts of *quaestiones* 5 and 6 and an interesting if incomplete discussion of them, see Jones, "Bede's Commentary on Genesis," pp. 147–51. Ray, "Venerable Bede," n. 159, gives further examples from Bede's works.

16. See Plummer I, pp. lx–lxi; Meyvaert, "Bede the Scholar," p. 46; and Jones's section on number symbolism in "Bede's Commentary on Genesis," pp. 166–74, and the bibliography on p. 166, n. 141.

17. *The Book of Rules of Tyconius* was well edited by F. C. Burkitt, Texts and Studies, no. 3 (Cambridge: Cambridge University Press, 1894). Augustine's version appears in *On Christian Doctrine* III.30–37, pp. 104–17. Thomas Mackay provides a critical edition of Bede's text, "Bede's Biblical Criticism: the Venerable Bede's Summary of Tyconius' *Liber Regularum*," in *Saints, Scholars, and Heroes*, ed. Margot H. King and Wesley M. Stevens (Collegeville, Minn.: St. John's Abbey and University, 1979) 1: 209–31. Jones treats it briefly in "Bede's Commentary on Genesis," pp. 145–46. Bonner deals with its importance and the influence of Tyconian commentary in *Saint Bede in the Tradition of Western Apocalyptic Commentary*.

18. Jones, "Bede's Commentary on Genesis," p. 146, cites *In Genesim* III. ll. 745–47, and *De tabernaculo* I, CCSL 119A, pp. 39–40, ll. 1355 ff.

19. See Laistner, *Hand-List*, pp. 20–78; Jones, Introduction to *In Genesim*, pp. vii–x; Meyvaert, "Bede the Scholar," pp. 63–64, n. 20. The works include *In Genesim* II–IV, *In Ezram et Neemiam, De tabernaculo, De templo, In Tobiam, In Marcum, Retractatio in Actus*, the final version of *De locis sanctis*, quite likely *Quaestiones XXX*, and perhaps *In Cantica*.

20. For the composition and structure of *In Genesim* see Charles W. Jones's introduction to his edition, CCSL 118A, pp. vi–x. For a consideration of Bede's commentary as an instructional manual in pastoral theology, see Judirh McClure, "Bede's *Notes on Genesis* and the Training of the Anglo-Saxon Clergy," in *The Bible in the Medieval World: Essays in Memory of Beryl Smalley*, ed. Katherine Walsh and Diana Wood (Oxford: Basil Blackwell, 1985), pp. 17–30. I am not convinced that Bede intended his commentaries to function primarily as pastoral training, but Dr. McClure has some important things to say about the structure and contents of this commentary on Genesis.

21. See Laistner, *Hand-List*, p. 70.

22. See Plummer I, p. cxlviii, n. 1: "In this work Bede's allegorical method appears in its greatest hardness; the determination to get an allegorical meaning at all hazards out of every passage leads to much forced artificiality." Also Laistner, *Hand-List*, p. 65; Carroll, *Venerable Bede*, p. 33.

23. Plummer, *HE* I, p. cl; Laistner, *Hand-List*, p. 75; CCSL 119A, praefatio, p. i.

24. Cited by Whitney F. Bolton, *A History of Anglo-Latin Literature, 597–1066* (Princeton, N.J.: Princeton University Press, 1967), I:127. Plummer refers to a number of quotations from *In Proverbia* in his discussion of Bede as a teacher, Introduction to *HE* I, pp. xxi–xxviii.

25. Salonius, *Commentarius in Parabolas Salomonis* (PL 53). For a list of seventy-five borrowings by Bede in his commentary, see CCSL 119B, pp. 468–69.

26. The four living creatures of Rev. 4:7 were for allegorical reasons variously assigned to the four evangelists; the lion, calf, man, eagle were, according to Irenaeus, John, Luke, Matthew, Mark; to Jerome, Mark, Matthew, Luke, and John; to Augustine (*De consensu evangelistarum* I.6), Matthew, Luke, Mark, and John; to others, still other configurations. Historically, Jerome's order has won the day, despite Augustine and Bede.

27. See Jeremy Cohen, "The Jews as Killers of Christ in the Latin Tradition, from Augustine to the Friars," *Traditio* 39 (1983): 1–27, esp. 10–12.

28. For the dating and sources of *Expositio* and *Retractatio,* see Laistner, *Bedae venerabilis expositio Actuum Apostolorum et retractatio* (Cambridge, Mass.: Mediaeval Academy of America, 1939), pp. xiii–xvii, xxxviii–xli. For Bede's mastery of Greek see Dionisotti, "On Bede, Grammars, and Greek," pp. 123–29, 140–41; and Kevin M. Lynch, "The Venerable Bede's Knowledge of Greek," *Traditio* 39 (1983): 432–39.

29. Glenn Olsen, "Bede as Historian: The Evidence from His Observations on the Life of the First Christian Community at Jerusalem," *Journal of Ecclesiastical History* 33 (1982): 519 and 530.

30. Concerning the text of the *Collectaneum,* see Laistner, *Hand-List,* pp. 37–38, mainly relying on André Wilmart, "La collection de Bède le vénérable sur l'Apôtre," *Revue Bénédictine* 38 (1926): 16–52; see also *Clavis patrum latinorum,* ed. E. Dekkers and A. Gaar, 2d ed., Sacris erudiri, no. 3 (1961), nos. 360, n., and 1360.

31. In his introduction to the translation of Bede's *Commentary on the Seven Catholic Epistles* (Kalamazoo, Mich.: Cistercian Publications, 1985), p. xv, Dom David Hurst says: "For some reason now difficult to fathom Bede chose the final part of the New Testament, the book of Acts, these seven Letters, and the Book of Revelation, when he first began his attempts at written exegesis of the books of sacred scripture early in the eighth century." Nevertheless, such a program is consistent with Bede's practice of furnishing texts on subjects that were very well known but needed simplifying and condensing or on subjects for which there were as yet no authorities on which the English could rely.

32. Laistner, *Hand-List,* pp. 30–31, and the long list of manuscripts, pp. 31–37.

33. On the extent and importance of Bede's contribution to the lapidary tradition and for a discussion of his sources of information, see Peter Kitson, "Lapidary Traditions in Anglo-Saxon England: Part II, Bede's *Explanatio Apocalypsis* and Related Works," *Anglo-Saxon England* 12

(1983):73–123. The translation of the quoted passage is by Kitson, p. 75, n. 9.

34. For a convenient summary of Lehmann's and Laistner's investigations see Laistner, *Hand-List,* pp. 155–57; also Jones, "Bede's Commentary on Genesis," pp. 115–98, esp. p. 147 and the references in n. 108.

35. On Bede's text, see Laistner, *Hand-List,* p. 83. The versions by Eucherius, Hegesippus and Adamnan from which Bede compiled his little book also appear in CSEL, vol. 39, ed. P. Geyer; other *itinera hierosolymitana* are published in CCSL 175. There is a more recent edition of Adamnan with an English translation: *Adamnan's De locis sanctis,* ed. Denis Meehan, Scriptores latini Hiberniae, no. 3 (Dublin: Dublin Institute for Advanced Studies, 1958). Meehan discusses Bede's version on pp. 3–6.

36. For the evidence on the authenticity of the glossary, see Laistner, *Bedae expositio et retractatio,* pp. xxxvii–viii.

Chapter Four

1. These two quotations may serve as a just sample of the praise accorded Bede's style:

Bede's command of Latin is excellent, and his style is clear and limpid, and it is very seldom that we have to pause to think of the meaning of a sentence. There is no affectation of a false classicality, and no touch of the puerile pomposity of his contemporary Aldhelm, for whom, however, he cannot help feeling a kind of admiration. Alcuin rightly praises Bede for his unpretending style. (Plummer I, pp. liii–liv)

But such is the pleasing simplicity, clarity, and grammatical superiority of his prose style that at least his narrative and historical works can be read with some aesthetic satisfaction. He habitually spoke, wrote, and taught in Latin all his life, so that there is a natural ease and directness in his prose which contrasts markedly with the rather 'showing-off' style of St Aldhelm, who perhaps wished to demonstrate that he could equal the Irish Latinists in stylistic learning. On the other hand, Bede's interest in metre, which produced his treatise *De Arte Metrica,* was due mainly to the value he set on the study of Latin metre as a necessary aid to the discipline of the effective use of that language. (C. L. Wrenn, *A Study of Old English Literature* [New York: Norton, 1967], p. 63)

2. Winthrop Weatherbee, "Some Implications of Bede's Latin Style," in *Bede and Anglo-Saxon England,* ed. Robert T. Farrell, British Archaeological Reports 46 (Oxford: British Archeological Reports, 1978), pp. 23–31, shows that Bede's style with its ease, purity, and freedom from self-

consciousness contributed to the development of a medieval Christian humanism.

3. See Alan Thacker, "Bede's Ideal of Reform," in *Ideal and Reality*, ed. Wormald, pp. 130–31.

4. For the summary results of Dom Germain Morin's researches into the original Bedan collection and of his own findings, consult Laistner, *Hand-List*, pp. 114–16. Reflecting the medieval accretions to Bede's collection and its confused order, the editions of Giles and Migne present a muddle. Indeed, one homily is printed twice as I.17 and II.24 in PL 94.89–96 and 262–67. Only the modern edition of Dom David Hurst, CCSL 120, is reliable for authenticity and order. For a list of the factitious homilies extracted from Bede's commentaries on Mark and Luke, see Hurst's appendix, pp. 381–84. For the dating of the collection, see his preface, p. vii.

5. On Bede's elaborate use of the metaphor of rumination, see Gernot Wieland, "Caedmon, the Clean Animal," *American Benedictine Review* 35 (1984):194–203, and the bibliography cited.

6. For a conspectus of his homiletic use of Scripture and the Fathers, see CCSL 120, Index Scriptorum, pp. 387–99 and 401–3.

7. See the two valuable but uneven articles on Bede's homiletic art by Philip J. West, "Liturgical Style and Structure in Bede's Homily for the Easter Vigil" and "Liturgical Style and Structure in Bede's Christmas Homilies," *American Benedictine Review* 23 (1972):1–8, 424–38. These are important because they are among the very few specific treatments of Bede's style. In making his point in the second article about the artistry of the sermon for midnight on Christmas (I.6), however, West belittles the form and treatment of the Vigil homily that precedes it (I.5), calling it "almost impoverished" (p. 425). West did not recognize that Bede is using two different methods, both artistic, for two different occasions: the one a simple reflection on the verses of the Gospel, echoing the simplicity of the mass text and spirit; the other, an elaborately structured and linguistically brilliant exposition for a brilliant night. West blames Bede for his procedure in the homily for the second mass, in which Bede "builds his sermon around allegorical interpretation of the Gospel's six main verbs: *transeamus, uideamus, uenerunt festinantes, uidentes, cognouerunt,* and *reuersi.* The sermon's limitation seems [sic] that this arbitrary organizational principal [sic] forced Bede to subordinate unity and continuity to ingenuity" (p. 432). West then praises Bede for holding allegory "to a minimum" in his sermon for Christmas Day (I.8). The arbitrariness is on the part of West, not Bede. If one appreciates Bede's (and the Fathers') allegorical art, then West's literary criticism appears perverse.

8. For a comprehensive survey of hagiography see René Aigrain, *L'hagiographie: ses sources, ses méthodes, son histoire* (Paris: Bloud & Gay, 1953).

For an understanding of the literary conventions used by hagiographers, see the studies by Hippolyte Delehaye, such as *The Legends of the Saints,* trans. Donald Attwater (New York: Fordham University Press, 1962), and *Les passions des martyrs et les genres littéraires,* 2d ed. (Brussels: Société des Bollandistes, 1966). For a still stimulating essay on hagiography, see chapter 4 in Charles W. Jones's *Saints' Lives and Chronicles in Early England* (Ithaca, N.Y.: Cornell University Press, 1947), pp. 51–79. For a summary of the influential Augustinian view of the miraculous, see Benedicta Ward, *Miracles and the Medieval Mind* (Philadelphia: University of Pennsylvania Press, 1982), introduction and chap. 1, pp. 1–4.

    9. On the development of the *opus geminatum* see, with the attendant bibliography, Peter Godman, "The Anglo-Latin *opus geminatum:* from Aldhelm to Alcuin," *Medium Aevum* 50, no. 2 (1981):215–29, and his edition of Alcuin, *The Bishops, Kings, and Saints of York,* pp. lxxviii–lxxxviii; and Gernot Wieland, "*Geminus Stilus:* Studies in Anglo-Latin Hagiography," in *Insular Latin Studies,* ed. Michael Herren (Toronto: Pontifical Institute of Medieval Studies, 1981), pp. 113–33. Wieland's study is particularly profitable for its explorations into the purposes and uses of the geminated format: "The conclusion to be drawn from this is not that the *gemina opera* were written to exemplify 'the interchangeability of metrical and non-metrical discourse,' but that the prose was written to complement the verse and the verse was written to complement the prose" (p. 125).

    10. Thomas W. Mackay has furnished us with an analysis of the work in his "A Critical Edition of Bede's Vita Felicis" (Ph.D. diss., Stanford University, 1971; Ann Arbor, Mich.: University Microfilms International, 1972), and in his article, "Bede's Hagiographical Method: His Knowledge and Use of Paulinus of Nola," in *Famulus Christi,* ed. Bonner, pp. 77–92. The factual details about the *Vita* and its source are drawn mainly from his introduction and article. Although I have studied his edition, my references will be to the text in Migne, since Mackay's edition is not yet available in CCSL.

    11. The best edition of the poems of Paulinus is *Sancti Pontii Meropii Paulini Nolani Carmina,* ed. Wilhelm von Hartel, CSEL 30 (Vienna: F. Tempsky, 1894). The *Natalicia* celebrating Felix are poems 12 to 29; the biography used by Bede is found in poems 15 and 16, the *Nachleben* especially in 18, and the buildings of Nola in 28. For a description and translation of the poems, see P. G. Walsh, *The Poems of St. Paulinus of Nola* (New York: Newman Press, 1975).

    12. In the preface to the prose life of St. Willibrord, Alcuin describes the purpose of the *opus geminatum* thus: "At your behest I have put together two small books, one moving along in prose, which could be read publicly to the brothers in church, if it seems worthy to your wisdom; the other, running along with Pierian feet, which ought only to be ruminated

by your students in the private room" (*Vita Willibrordi archiepiscopi Traiectensis*, ed. W. Levinson, MGH, Scriptores rerum Merowingicarum VII.113).

13. See Mackay, Introduction to his critical edition, pp. xxv–lxi, esp. liii–liv, and "Bede's Hagiographical Method," p. 78; Hunter Blair, *World of Bede*, pp. 119–20.

14. Carmelo V. Franklin and Paul Meyvaert, "Has Bede's Version of the 'Passio S. Anastasii' Come Down to Us in 'BHL' 408?" *Analecta Bollandiana* 100 (1982):373–400. BHL 408 refers to *Bibliotheca hagiographica latina*, ed. Socii Bollandiani (Bruxelles, Belgium: Bollandists, 1898–99)1:68, no. 408.

15. Franklin and Meyvaert, "Bede's Version," 394–95.

16. The most damning censure was leveled by Bede's ablest and kindest critic, Charles Plummer:

In the case of Cuthbert's Life it cannot, I think, be said that Bede has bettered his original. He has improved the Latinity no doubt, and made the whole thing run more smoothly. In fact he seems to take delight in altering the language for the mere sake of alteration, while keeping closely to the sense. But he has obliterated many interesting details of time and place, he shows a marked tendency to exaggerate the ascetic and miraculous element, he amplifies the narrative with rhetorical matter which can only be called padding, inserts as facts explanations of his own, and has greatly spoiled one beautiful anecdote. On the other hand, his account of Cuthbert's death, derived from an eye-witness, is of real and independent value. (p. xlvi)

For the others, see the remarks and documentation in Lenore Abraham, "Bede's *Life of Cuthbert:* A Reassessment," *Proceedings of the Patristic, Medieval, and Renaissance Conference* 1 (1976):23–24.

17. On the narrative qualities of the anonymous *Vita Cuthberti* see Theodor Wolpers, *Die englische Heiligenlegende des Mittelalters*, Buchreihe der *Anglia*, no. 10 (Tübingen, Germany: Max Niemeyer, 1964), pp. 74–75.

18. Augustine, *On Christian Doctrine* IV.19.38, p. 146. Cf. Wieland, "*Geminus stilus*," pp. 124–26.

19. J. F. Webb, ed. and trans. *Lives of the Saints* (Harmondsworth, England, and Baltimore: Penguin, 1981), p. 23. Webb's introduction to Bede's prose life is an excellent rebuttal to Plummer's opinion quoted in n. 6 above.

20. On the dating from this reference, see Max Manitius, *Geschichte der lateinischen Literatur des Mittelalters*, Handbuch der Altertumswissenschaft, ed. Walter Otto, sec. 9, part 2 (Munich, Germany: C. H. Beck, 1911; rpt. 1965), 1:84; and Werner Jaager, *Bedas metrische vita sancti*

Cuthberti, Palaestra 198 (Leipzig, Germany: Mayer and Müller, 1935), p. 4.

21. On the word *curatio* see *Thesaurus linguae latinae,* IV. 1476–77. For a discussion of the various understandings of Bede's gift in both the medieval and modern periods, see Whitelock, "Bede and his Teachers and Friends," p. 21 and nn. 15–21.

22. See Jaager's introduction and statistics, pp. 2–3, and B. Colgrave's concordance of the three lives, in *Two Lives of St. Cuthbert,* ed. and trans. Colgrave (Cambridge: Cambridge University Press, 1940), p. 375.

23. Jaager's three brief references to Virgil's *Georgics* in this passage, I.244 (should read I.224) and II.14 for lines 415 and 16 and I.509 for 423 do not at all convey the amount of Virgilian imitation in the passage. Cf., for example, *Georgics* I.50 and 111; I.219–24; II.237; IV.158; *Aeneid* VII.721; XI.301. As for the mock-epic quality, note that *dixerat,* l. 426, is used by Virgil for epic discourse twenty-five times in the *Aeneid,* but never in the *Eclogues* or *Georgics.* For Bede's use of Virgil in the metrical life, see further Neil Wright, "Bede and Vergil," *Romanobarbarica* 6 (1981):363, 367–71.

24. For a discussion of the peculiarities of this monachism see A. Hamilton Thompson, "Northumbrian Monasticism," in *Bede: His Life, Times, and Writings,* pp. 60–101, esp. p.72; and Colgrave's n., p. 347.

25. See Jaager, *Bedas metrische Vita,* pp. 24–32; Colgrave, *Two Lives,* pp. 17–50; Laistner, *Hand-List,* pp. 88–90.

26. For text and translation, unfortunately without commentary, of three accounts of the two sea otters wiping and warming Cuthbert's feet, see Bolton, *Anglo-Latin Literature,* pp. 136–38.

27. Dom Henri Quentin, *Les martyrologes historiques du moyen âge,* 2d ed. (Paris: Lecoffre, 1908), in a brilliant scholarly enterprise in chap. 2 (pp. 17–119) presents Bede's contribution to the martyrological genre. The martyrology itself is now in a convenient form, *Edition practique des martyrologes de Bède, de l'anonyme lyonnais, et de Florus,* ed. Dom Jacques DuBois and Geneviève Renaud (Paris: CNRS, 1976).

28. The main contributors before the fixing of the *Roman Martyrology* were the ninth-century writers Florus of Lyons, Hrabanus, Ado, and Usuard. The composite jumble is represented by the martyrology printed with Bede's works in PL 94.799–1148. Until a new edition appears, only Quentin's is reliable.

29. The usually careful Laistner has misled a number of later scholars about the history of these books. In the *Hand-List* he avers: "Neither of these collections of poems has survived as such, but, according to John Boston of Bury, the library of Bury St Edmunds early in the fifteenth century had a *Liber Hymnorum* and a *Liber Epigrammatum* bearing Bede's name" (p. 122). Richard H. Rouse, "Bostonus Buriensis and the Author

of the *Catalogus Scriptorum Ecclesiae,*" *Speculum* 41 (1966):471–99, demonstrated that Bostonus Buriensis was only the scribe of the catalogue and Henry of Kirkestede, subprior and librarian, was the author; but Rouse also made clear that Kirkestede's catalogue was not an actual catalogue of library holdings but a bio-bibliographic union catalogue which comprised a list of all the books by authoritative and approved authors that Kirkestede knew of and wished to get if they were not yet available (pp. 471–72, 493–94). It is clear that Kirkestede learned about Bede's works from Bede's own bibliography, which he copied in the same order and wording as found in *HE* V.24 (pp. 566–71). That neither Bury St. Edmunds nor the Franciscan convents or neighboring monasteries possessed Bede's poems is manifest from the fact that Kirkestede was unable to supply an incipit and explicit for the works nor a reference number for the location (see p. 496, items 40 and 41). Laistner's misunderstanding of the nature of the list has been repeated by recent, also usually careful, scholars. Michael Lapidge, for instance, in "Some Remnants of Bede's Lost *Liber Epigrammatum,*" *English Historical Review* 90 (1975):798, states that a copy of the book of epigrams "was known to Henry of Kirkestede."

30. On the alphabetic and reciprocal form, see Plummer II, 241. Bede cites the well-known accentual alphabetic poem, *Apparebit repentina* in *De arte metrica* I.24, p. 139. Ernst Robert Curtius, *European Literature and the Latin Middle Ages,* trans. Willard R. Trask (New York: Pantheon, 1953), pp. 235–36, identifies and describes the use of the topos, which he labeled "contrast between pagan and Christian poetry." Bede would be familiar with it from his reading in Juvencus, Paulinus of Nola, and Paulinus of Périgueux.

31. Anyone using the Fraipont edition should pay attention to Walther Bulst's learned, scathing critique of it, "Bedae Opera Rhythmica?" *Zeitschrift für deutsches Altertum und deutsche Literatur* 89 (1958–59):83–91. My remarks on the form and contents of the CCSL edition draw on his expertise, as well as on the learning of Josef Szövérffy, *Die Annalen der lateinischen Hymnendichtung* (Berlin: Erich Schmidt, 1966), 1:168–76.

32. G. M. Dreves, *Lateinische Hymnendichter des Mittelalters,* Analecta hymnica medii aevi, 50 (Leipzig, Germany, 1907, reprint ed. New York: Johnson Reprint, 1961), p. 98, takes over eleven hymns attributed to Bede in George Cassander's Renaissance collection from a tenth-century manuscript but adds another four, including the two hymns, from manuscript Bamberg B.II.10, among the hymn fragments without authorial ascription, found next to hymns attributed to Bede. As Bulst expostulates, that is no good reason to ascribe these two to Bede, which are, moreover, "dürftig, plump und mühselig zusammengestückt"; they could be by any of a dozen hymn writers (Bulst, "Bedae Opera Rhythmica?" pp. 88–89).

33. For a description of the *hymni Ambrosiani,* see F. J. E. Raby, *A*

History of Christian-Latin Poetry, from the Beginnings to the Close of the Middle Ages, 2d ed. (Oxford: Clarendon Press, 1966), pp. 28–41, esp. p. 33.

34. See A. S. Walpole, *Early Latin Hymns* (Cambridge: Cambridge University Press, 1922; reprint ed., 1966), pp. 371–76. Walpole's book with its excellent introduction and notes remains the best introductory text for the early hymns.

35. See Daniel G. Calder, *Cynewulf,* (Boston: G. K. Hall, 1981), chap. 3, pp. 42–74; and George H. Brown, "The Descent-Ascent Motif in *Christ II* of Cynewulf," *Journal of English and Germanic Philology* 73 (1974):1–12. A. S. Cook suggested a relationship between Bede's and Cynewulf's poems in his edition of *The Christ of Cynewulf* (Boston: Ginn & Co., 1909), pp. 116–18.

36. M. Bonnet, ed., *Acta Apostolorum Apocrypha* II.1 (Leipzig, Germany: Hermann Mendelssohn, 1898), pp. 24–26. See the notes, particularly to verses 39a, 42a, 87–89a, of *The Dream of the Rood* in *Bright's Old English Grammar & Reader,* ed. Frederick G. Cassidy and Richard N. Ringler, 3d ed. (New York: Holt, Rinehart, & Winston, 1971), pp. 309–17; also *The Dream of the Rood,* ed. Michael Swanton (Manchester, England: University Press; New York: Barnes & Noble, 1970), pp. 42–78.

37. The poem was edited with an English translation by J. Rawson Lumby as *Be Domes Dæge, De Die Judicii,* Early English Text Society Original Series, no. 65 (London: Trübner, 1876). The best edition of the poem, titled *Judgment Day II,* is in the *Anglo-Saxon Poetic Records,* ed. E. V. K. Dobbie, Vol. 6 (New York: Columbia University Press, 1942); the most recent English translation is that by S. A. J. Bradley, *Anglo Saxon Poetry* (London: Dent, 1982), pp. 528–35. An Old English prose adaptation of *Judgment Day II* appears as part of sermon xxix in *Wulfstan, Sammlung der ihm zugeschriebenen Homilien nebst Untersuchungen über ihre Echtheit,* ed. A. S. Napier, (Berlin, 1883; reprint ed. with bibliographic appendix by Klaus Ostheeren, Zürich: Weidmann, 1967)*,* 1:vi, 136–40. Both Bede's Latin text and the Old English versions have been the subject of extensive investigation over the years by Leslie Whitbread, in preparation for a new, needed (but unfortunately not forthcoming) edition. All Bedan and Old English research is indebted to his research, reported in a series of articles, of which the following pertain to the Latin poem: "A Study of Bede's *Versus De Die Iudicii,*" *Philological Quarterly* 23 (1944):194–221; "Note on a Bede Fragment," *Scriptorium* 12 (1958):280–81; "The Sources and Literary Qualities of Bede's Doomsday Verses," *Zeitschrift für deutsches Altertum und deutsche Literatur* 95 (1966):258–66; "The Old English Poem *Judgment Day II* and its Latin Source," *Philological Quarterly* 45 (1966):635–56; "Bede's Verses on Doomsday: A Supplemental Note," *Philological Quarterly* 51 (1972):485–86; "After Bede: The Influence and Dissemination of His Doomsday Verses," *Archiv* 204 (1967):250–66. For

further information about the Old English versions one should consult
Stanley B. Greenfield and Daniel G. Calder, *A New Critical History of Old
English Literature* (New York: New York University Press, 1986), pp.238–
40, and for bibliography on the OE poem, see *A Bibliography of Publications
on Old English to the End of 1972,* ed. Greenfield and Fred C. Robinson
(Toronto: Toronto University Press, 1979); thereafter, the annual bibliographies in *Anglo-Saxon England* and the *PMLA*.

38. For Whitbread's final and best argued grounds for attributing
the poem to Bede, see his "After Bede," 251–54. Mabillon's remark, "nec
Bedae venam assequi mihi videtur" ("this does not seem to me to follow
the vein of Bede") found in PL 120.22, is cited in Whitbread's n. 4,
along with the opinions of most critics for and against Bede's authorship.
The attribution of the poem to Alcuin, often repeated in OE scholarship
from Lumby's remark in the preface, pp. v–vi, is due to a chance juxtapostion of the poem next to one atrributed to Alcuin in Vienna, MS 89
(See Whitbread, "After Bede," p. 251 and n. 3).

39. Raby, *Christian-Latin Poetry*, p. 148. In his and James L. Rosier's
edition of Aldhelm, *The Poetic Works* (Cambridge, England: D.S. Brewer,
1985), p. 31, Michael Lapidge boldly brands Raby's hitherto revered study
"a tissue of errors and wrong-headed opinions."

40. For a list and location of most of the poems atributed to Bede,
see Bolton, *Anglo-Latin Literature*, pp. 167–68. To this should be added
the two epigrams from John Leland's *De rebus brittanicis collectanea,* ed.
Thomas Hearne, 2d ed. (London: Benjamin White, 1774), 3:114–15,
printed by Lapidge, "Some Remnants," as nos. 2 and 10 (pp. 802, 805);
and an eleven-line epigram assocated with the preface to Bede's commentary on the Apocalypse (see Laistner, *Hand-List,* p. 129).

41. See Michael Lapidge, "Some Remnants of Bede's Lost *Liber Epigrammatum,*" pp. 798–820, with transcript of the epigrams on pp. 802–
6. A notation by Leland about *Enigmata Bedae* as part of this manuscript
suggests that Bede like Aldhelm and Tatwin authored *aenigmata* (learned
riddles) (*Collectanea,* 3:114; Lapidge, "Remnants," p. 803).

42. Patrick Sims-Williams, "Milred of Worcester's Collection of Latin
Epigrams and its Continental Counterparts," *Anglo-Saxon England* 10
(1982):38.

43. On this text Colgrave remarks, *HE,* pp. 580–81, n. 4, "Only
a comparatively small group of the MSS. of the Letter attribute the composition of the poem to Bede himself, and those the later ones." See Dobbie,
The Manuscripts of Cædmon's Hymn and Bede's Death Song. A. H. Smith's
statement in his edition of *Three Northumbrian Poems*, rev. ed. (Exeter,
England: University of Exeter Press, 1978), p. 17, "On Cuthbert's testimony the Death Song is Bede's," is certainly not valid without qualification. He includes the Latin phrases of the earlier and later manuscript

recensions on pp. 41–43. See also Michael W. Twomey, "On Reading 'Bede's Death Song': Translation, Typology, and Penance in Symeon of Durham's Text of the 'Epistola Cuthberti de Obitu Bedae,' " *Neuphilologische Mitteilungen* 84 (1983):171–81.

44. Concerning the content of the letter, see *Bedae opera de temporibus,* ed. Jones, pp. 132–35. Both Jones and Bolton (in *Anglo-Latin Literature,* p. 151) mistranslate a portion of the letter, so that the David whom he asks to come to his aid becomes the original perpetrator of the accusation against Bede. See Dieter Schaller, "Der verleumdete David: zum Schlußkapitel von Bedas 'Epistola ad Pleguinam,' " *Literatur und Sprache im europäischen Mittelalter: Festschrift für Karl Langosch,* ed. Alf Önnerfors, Johannes Rathofer, Fritz Wagner (Darmstadt, Germany: Wissenschaftliche Buchgesellschaft, 1973), pp. 39–43.

45. This letter exists only in a printed version transcribed from a now lost manuscript of the monastery of St. Vincent in Metz, published by Jean Mabillon in *Vetera analecta* (Paris: Montalant, 1723; reprint ed., Farnborough, England: Gregg, 1967), p. 398. No known manuscript contains it. See Laistner, *Hand-List,* p. 119.

46. See Plummer II, pp. 1–2; Levison, "Bede as Historian," p. 128.

47. See Thacker, "Bede's Ideal of Reform," pp. 130–53.

48. For a summary of Bede's protests against clerical abuses, see the texts cited by Plummer I, p. xxxv, and II, pp. 381–86.

49. The abusive system of founding familial *monasteriola* under the rule and control of a family member as abbot or abbess was, according to Bede, already in existence for thirty years, since King Aldfrith's days. It was also widespread on the Continent. When Egbert and Eadbert attempted to put Bede's recommendation into effect, they incurred papal displeasure (see *EHD* I, no. 184). The abuse was again attacked by the tenth-century Benedictine reformers.

50. See Jan Davidse's thoughtful analysis in "The Sense of History in the Works of the Venerable Bede," *Studi medievali,* 3d ser., 23 (1982):668–70.

51. Davidse, "Sense of History," p. 670, justifiably calls in question the tone of Bede's swan song as interpreted by John Smith (1722), Plummer II, p. 378, and Musca, *Il venerabile Beda,* p. 345.

Chapter Five

1. Edited by Plummer I, pp. 388–404, with notes in II, pp. 371–77, the *Life of Ceolfrith* has been translated by Douglas Samuel Boutflower, *The Life of Ceolfrid* (Sunderland, England: Hills & Co., 1912); Clinton Albertson, *Anglo-Saxon Saints and Heroes* (New York: Fordham University Press, 1967), pp. 247–71; and Dorothy Whitelock, *EHD* I, pp. 758–

70. For a summary analysis of its contents and worth, see Levison, "Bede as Historian," pp. 129–31. The life is so well done that Dorothy Whitelock was tempted to consider Bede the author (see her "Bede and His Teachers and Friends," pp. 20–22), and Judith McClure has made a very strong case for doing so ("Bede and the Life of Ceolfrid," *Peritia* 3 (1984): 71–84; others have suggested Hwætberht or one of Bede's students as author (Bertram Colgrave, "The Earliest Saints' Lives Written in England," *Proceedings of the British Academy* 44 (1958):58).

2. See *Bedae opera de temporibus*, ed. Jones, pp. 120–22.

3. I am indebted for this suggestive historical explanation to Roger Ray in his forthcoming article on Bede in the series *Aufstieg und Niedergang der römischen Welt*.

4. For a review of the scholarship and findings on how dependent the *Anglo-Saxon Chronicle* was on Bede, see Janet Bately, "Bede and the Anglo-Saxon Chronicle," in *Saints, Scholars, and Heroes*, 1:233–54.

5. "The popularity of the *HE* on the European Continent is very striking and makes the view sometimes expressed, that this work interested only the English, look very foolish." Laistner, *Hand-List*, p. 94.

6. See Arnaldo Momigliano, "Pagan and Christian Historiography in the Fourth Century A.D.," *The Conflict between Paganism and Christianity in the Fourth Century*, ed. Momigliano (Oxford: Clarendon Press, 1963), pp. 79–99; J. Campbell, "Bede," pp. 162–65; R. A. Markus, *Bede and the Tradition of Ecclesiastical Historiography*, Jarrow Lecture 1975.

7. See Michael Richter, "Bede's *Angli:* Angles or English?" *Peritia* 3 (1984): 99–114.

8. For the convention of the exordial topoi see Roger Ray, "Bede's *Vera Lex Historiae*," *Speculum* 55 (1980):11–12, and the authorities listed in n. 51. For Bede's artful joining of a "formula of submission" with a "devotional formula" in his address to King Ceolwulf, see Kendall, "Bede's *Historia ecclesiastica*," p. 151.

9. See James Campbell, *Bede's Reges and Principes*, Jarrow Lecture 1979; and the same author's "Bede," pp. 168–72; J. M. Wallace-Hadrill, "Bede," in *Early Germanic Kingship*, pp. 72–97, and his "Gregory of Tours and Bede: Their Views on the Personal Qualities of Kings," *Frühmittelalterliche Studien* 2 (1968):31–44; Hans-Joachim Diesner, "Incarnationsjahre, 'Militia Christi,' und anglische Königsporträts bei Beda Venerabilis," *Mittellateinisches Jahrbuch* 16 (1981):17–34; also Antonia Gransden's chapter on Bede in *Historical Writing in England c. 550 to c. 1307* (Ithaca, N.Y.: Cornell University Press, 1975), pp. 13–28, esp. 22.

10. For one modern historian's speculation on royal advantages in cooperating with Anglo-Saxon clerics, see Richard Abels, "The Council of Whitby: A Study in Early Anglo-Saxon Politics," *Journal of British Studies* 23, no. 1 (1983):1–25.

11. Concerning Ceolwulf's forcible tonsure in 731 and voluntary monasticism in 737 see Colgrave's note to the preface of *HE*, p. 2; Plummer II, p. 340. For the phenomenon of seventh-and eighth-century kings who abdicated in order to become monks or pilgrims, see Stancliffe, "Kings Who Opted Out," pp. 154–76.

12. Again, Alan Thacker is particularly acute in identifying and analyzing the grounds for this idealization in *HE:* "Bede's Ideal of Reform," pp. 136–49. See also Wormald, "Bede and Benedict Biscop," pp. 155–56.

13. See Colgrave, *HE,* p. xxxi; Campbell, "Bede," pp. 163–64; Levison, "Bede as Historian," pp. 134–37.

14. See Donald K. Fry's "The Art of Bede II: the Reliable Narrator as Persona," in *The Early Middle Ages,* Acta, no. 6 (Binghamton: SUNY Press, 1982), pp. 63–82.

15. Bede took the term from another context and meaning, Jerome's defense against Helvidius of the Evangelists' calling Joseph the father of Jesus, asserting that they were simply "expressing the common opinion, which is a true law of history." See the important article by Ray, "Bede's *Vera Lex Historiae.*" He corrects Jones's mistaken interpretation of Jerome in *Saints' Lives and Chronicles,* p. 83, and shows that Bede inserted this phrase to counter Isidore's opinion that common report was inadmissable for historical evidence.

16. Colgrave, *HE,* ed. Colgrave and Mynors, p. xxx; J. N. Stephens, "Bede's Ecclesiastical History," *History* 62 (1977): 1–14. Stephens's article contains valuable insights into the nature of *HE* and corrects some commonly accepted theses about it. But, by inquiring "may we not suppose that Bede would also have wished for [the *History*] to end with the *gens Anglorum* triumphant in all Britain, perhaps by arms and certainly by religion?" (p. 9), Stephens attributes to Bede a theological triumphalism alien to him. Bede was too much a realist and an Augustinian to insist on being "able to draw his work to a nice conclusion of matching proportions" (p. 9; see also pp. 10–12).

17. On chronological and factual mistakes detectable in *HE* see Campbell, "Bede," pp. 165–67; D. P. Kirby, "Bede and Northumbrian Chronology," *English Historical Review* 78 (1963): 514–27, and his "Bede's Native Sources for the *Historia ecclesiastica,*" *Bulletin of the John Rylands Library* 48 (1966): 341–71; Patrick Sims-Williams, "The Settlement of England in Bede and the *Chronicle,*" *Anglo-Saxon England* 12 (1983): 1–41. On the other hand, the precise scholar Kenneth Harrison in *The Framework of Anglo-Saxon History to* A.D. *900* (Cambridge University Press, 1976), pp. 76–98, examines Bede's dating carefully and asserts that the "main sequence of dates from 596 to 729 appears to be reliable and free of systematic error" (p. 96).

18. Donald K. Fry, "Bede Fortunate in His Translator: The Barking Nuns," in *Studies in Earlier Old English Prose*, ed. Szarmach, pp. 345–46.

19. T. M. Charles-Edwards, "Bede, the Irish and the Britons," *Celtica* 15 (1983):42–52, explains Bede's hostility to the Britons for failing to preach to the English, whereas the Irish, who did not lack charity, preached to the English and eventually saw their error in opposing the Roman church on Easter dating.

20. See Paul Meyvaert, "Bede's Text of the *Libellus responsionum* of Gregory the Great to Augustine of Canterbury," in *England before the Conquest: Studies in Primary Sources Presented to Dorothy Whitelock*, ed. P. Clemoes and K. Hughes (Cambridge: Cambridge University Press, 1971), pp. 15–33; and for Bede's respect for Gregory, see *Bede and Gregory the Great*, both reprinted in *Benedict, Gregory, Bede and Others*, as items IX and X.

21. Plummer remarks that this is an awkward chapter that would have come in better before II.9 (II.64), and that there is no natural reason for dividing the books here (II, pp. 66–67). Stephens, "Bede's Ecclesiastical History," p. 11, rejects Colgrave's suggestion, *HE*, ed. Colgrave and Mynors, p. 116, n. 1, that the chapter may have been influenced by an Old English heroic poem; he instead urges that Æthelfrith was "merely a convenient example of the Old Testament of the *gens Anglorum*."

22. The modern chapter numbering of book IV, chapters 14–30, are two ahead of the authentic text because of one early added chapter and one later divided chapter. See n., p. 236, *HE*, ed. Colgrave and Mynors.

23. On Cædmon's Hymn, see Stanley B. Greenfield and Daniel G. Calder, *A New Critical History of Old English Literature* (New York: New York University Press, 1986), pp. 227–31. John C. Pope, ed., *Seven Old English Poems*, 2d ed. (New York: Norton, 1981), pp. 3–4, gives, as do other Old English readers, both the Northumbrian version of Cædmon's Hymn from the Moore and Leningrad manuscripts and a West Saxon Version; Pope also provides an excellent commentary, pp. 45–54. On the manuscript tradition, see Mynors, *HE*, pp. xxxix–lxx, and Colgrave's note, p. 417, supplemented by K. W. Humphreys and Alan A. C. Ross, "Further Manuscripts of Bede's 'Historia Ecclesiastica,' of the 'Epistola Cuthberti de Obitu Bedae,' and Further Anglo-Saxon Texts of 'Cædmon's Hymn' and 'Bede's Death Song,' " *Notes and Queries* n.s. 22 (1975): 52–53. Concerning the topos of *ruminatio*, see André Crépin, "Bede and the Vernacular," in *Famulus Christi*, ed. G. Bonner, pp. 172–73; Philip J. West, "Ruminations in Bede's Account of Cædmon," *Monastic Studies* 12 (1976): 217–36; and Gernot Wieland, "Cædmon, the Clean Animal," *American Benedictine Review* 35 (1984): 194–203. Scholars have wondered why Bede went to the trouble of giving a paraphrase in Latin of Cædmon's Hymn with an excuse for the loss of poetry in the translation when he

could have easily inserted the original Old English nine-line poem into his text, as indeed numerous copyists did. From this account of Cædmon as well as from information in Cuthbert's Letter about Bede's own knowledge and use of the vernacular, it is clear that Bede was not hostile to Old English Christian verse. In "Cædmon and Christian Poetry," *Neuphilologische Mitteilungen* 84 (1983), 163–70, P. R. Orton wonders whether perhaps "Bede suppressed the *Hymn* because its conventional qualities proclaim its debt to previous tradition so clearly as to undermine the story's claim that Cædmon's gift owed nothing to men and everything to grace" (p. 169).

24. For the influence of exegesis on Bede's historiography, see Davidse, "Sense of History," pp. 647–95, with the bibliography cited in nn. 6, 11, 12, 33, 106; Roger D. Ray, "Bede, the Exegete, as Historian," in *Famulus Christi,* ed. Bonner, pp. 125–40, and his "Augustine's *De Consensu Evangelistarum* and the Historical Education of the Venerable Bede," *Studia Patristica* 16 (1984):555–61; Robert W. Hanning, *The Vision of History in Early Britain* (New York: Columbia University Press, 1966).

25. Even Levison took this attitude in the still seminal "Bede as Historian," pp. 122–23, 144, 147. Henry Mayr-Harting in his review of *Famulus Christi* pointed out that "one of the significant advances of 1976 over 1935 is the appreciation of how Bede's scriptural scholarship affected, indeed permeated, his work as an historian." *Journal of Ecclesiastical History* 29 (1978):363. See Davidse, "Sense of History," 648–49.

26. In this section I make use especially of Joel T. Rosenthal, "Bede's Use of Miracles in 'The Ecclesiastical History,' " *Traditio* 31 (1975):328–35, and Meyvaert, "Bede the Scholar," pp. 51–54. See also Bertram Colgrave, "Bede's Miracle Stories," in *Bede, His Life, Times, and Writings,* ed. Thompson, pp. 201–29; also "The Earliest Saints' Lives Written in England," *Proceedings of the British Academy* 44 (1958):35–60, and *HE,* pp. xxxiv–xxxvi.

Chapter Six

1. Letter 216, *Alcuini epistolae,* MGH, p. 360.
2. See Whitelock, *After Bede,* pp. 4–5.
3. See Parkes, *The Scriptorium of Wearmouth-Jarrow,* pp. 15–22.
4. See Friedrich Wiegand, *Das Homiliarium Karls des Grossen* (Leipzig: A. Deichert, 1897), pp. 79–80; for other homiliaries containing a large assortment of Bede's homilies, see Reginald Grégoire, *Les homéliaires du moyen âge: inventaire et analyse des manuscrits* (Rome: Herder, 1966). A homiliary is a collection of sermons for the liturgical year to be used either at mass or in the office.

5. Colgrave, *Two Lives of Saint Cuthbert*, p. 351; and his "Earliest Saints' Lives," pp. 51–55.

6. Alcuin, *The Bishops, Kings, and Saints of York*, ed. Godman, pp. xlviii–liii, lxxxviii, xci, and elsewhere (see index, pp. 145–46; 191–92); Whitelock, "After Bede," p. 7.

7. Quoted by Próinséas ní Chatháin, "Bede's Ecclesiastical History in Irish," *Peritia* 3 (1984): 119. For Alcuin's association of Bede with the Fathers, see Alcuin, *The Bishops, Kings, and Saints of York*, ed. Godman, vv. 1536–47, and n. to l. 1547, pp. 123–24. For Claudius of Turin, see his preface to *Enarratio in epistolam d. Pauli ad Galatas*, PL 104.835C. For the Council of Aachen see MGH *Concilia* II.759.

8. William of Malmesbury "recognized Bede as the only 'professional' historian of Anglo-Saxon times. The influence of Bede on him is very evident." Gransden, *Historical Writing*, p. 169. For Bede's influence on English medieval historiography, see Gransden's very informative article, "Bede's Reputation as an Historian in Medieval England," *Journal of Ecclesiastical History* 32 (1981): 397–425.

9. Still the best scholarly analysis of the Old English Bede and of the various claims for its authorship is Dorothy Whitelock's "The Old English Bede," *Proceedings of the British Academy* 48 (1962); reprint ed. in *From Bede to Alfred* (London: Variorum, 1980), item VIII. The statement that Ælfric makes in his homily on Saint Gregory that "King Ælfred translated Bede's *Historia Anglorum* from Latin into English" cannot be right. *Ælfric's Catholic Homilies: The Second Series*, ed. Malcolm Godden (Oxford: EETS, 1979), p. 72, l. 71–72.

10. *Critical History*, p. 32. See his and Calder's *New Critical History*, pp. 57–58. See also Fry, "Bede Fortunate," pp. 345–62; Whitelock, "The Old English Bede," 57–90, and her "The Prose of Alfred's Reign," in *Continuations and Beginnings*, ed. E. G. Stanley (London: Nelson, 1966), the latter articles also reprinted in *From Bede to Alfred*.

11. Laistner, "Bede as a Scholar," p. 115; see also his *Hand-List*, pp. 20–82, esp. the chart on p. 5, for a listing of the manuscripts known to him in 1943. Many more have since been noticed by scholars and incorporated into the critical apparatus of the CCSL editions.

12. See Laistner, *Hand-List*, for the list and description of the manuscripts of *HA* (pp. 112–13) and *HE* (pp. 93–111); R. A. B. Mynors furnishes further information on MSS of *HE* in his and Colgrave's edition of *HE*, pp. xxxix–lxx; this has been supplemented by Humphreys and Ross, "Further Manuscripts," pp. 50–52. Mynors notes, "Bede's *History* is one of the very few works written in Latin before the Carolingian renaissance which have come down to us in copies virtually contemporary with their authors; the scribes of our two oldest manuscripts might well

have been among the disciples who gathered round the master's deathbed" (p. xxxix).

Facsimiles of the two oldest manuscripts, Cambridge, University Library Kk. 5. 16 (the Moore MS), and Leningrad, Public Library Lat. Q. v. I. 18, are published in the series Early English Manuscripts in Facsimile, vols. 9 (1959), ed. Peter Hunter Blair, and 2 (1952), ed. O. Arngart.

13. Laistner, "Was Bede the Author of a Penitential?" in *The Intellectual Heritage of the Early Middle Ages*, pp. 165–66.

14. See Charles W. Jones, *Bedae Pseudepigrapha: Scientific Writings Falsely Attributed to Bede* (Ithaca, N.Y.: Cornell University Press, 1939), pp. vii and 48–94; *Clavis patrum latinorum*, 2d ed., *Sacris Erudiri*, no. 3 (1961), nos. 635, 1384, 2282–83, and index, p. 532; Bolton, *Anglo-Latin Literature*, pp. 184–85.

15. Alcuin, *Bishops, Kings, and Saints of York*, ed. Godman, pp. 103–4. That miracle is, as Godman notes, significantly similar to one of Saint Cuthbert's described in vv. 733–34.

16. For the veneration paid to Bede as a saint, see Carroll, *Venerable Bede*, pp. 56–63.

17. For a brief picture essay on Saint Cuthbert's tomb, see *The Anglo-Saxons*, ed. Campbell, pp. 80–81; for further information, see C. F. Battiscombe, *The Relics of St. Cuthbert* (Oxford: Oxford University Press, 1956). On the theft of Bede's body and the honor paid his relics, see C. E. Whiting, "The Life of the Venerable Bede," in *Bede, His Life, Times, and Writings*, ed. Thompson, pp. 37–38.

18. R. W. Chambers, "Bede," *Proceedings of the British Academy* 22 (1936):151.

19. A notable exception is the preeminent Renaissance biblical scholar Erasmus, who dismissed Bede as completely derivative. Others, without looking very carefully at what Bede does on his own in his commentaries, have formed the same low opinion.

20. Paul Meyvaert makes this point well in *Bede the Scholar*, pp. 53–56; reprint ed. in *Benedict, Gregory, Bede and Others* (London: Variorum Reprints, 1977)

21. Plummer, *HE* I, pp. lxxviii–lxxix, calls Bede "the very model of the saintly-scholar priest." See J. M. Wallace-Hadrill, "Bede and Plummer," in *Famulus Christi*, ed. Bonner, pp. 366–85.

22. Abbie Findlay Potts, ed., *The Ecclesiastical Sonnets of William Wordsworth: A Critical Edition* (New Haven, Conn.: Yale University Press, 1922), p. 117 (Wordsworth's Advertisement of 1822) and p. 131 (the sonnet). After finishing this book, the reader might especially enjoy the sonnets of the first book, since they pertain to Anglo-Saxon England and Bede's *History*.

Selected Bibliography

Note: For more detailed bibliography on particular topics consult the notes to the pertinent chapters.

PRIMARY SOURCES

1. Collected Works

The Complete Works of the Venerable Bede in the Original Latin . . . Accompanied by a New English Translation of the Historical Works. Edited by J. A. Giles. 12 vols. London: Whitaker & Co., 1843–44.

Bedae venerabilis opera. Various editors. Corpus Christianorum Series Latina (CCSL). Vols. 118–20, 122–23, 175–76, to date. Turnhout, Belgium: Brepols, 1960–83.

Venerabilis Bedae Opera Omnia. Edited by J.-P. Migne. Patrologia Latina (PL). Vols. 90–95. Paris: J.-P. Migne, 1850–51. Reprint. Turnhout, Belgium: Brepols, 1980. The editions of Giles and Migne are unreliable. The student should use a recent critical edition such as the CCSL if one is available. The CCSL is not yet complete.

2. Educational Treatises

Metrics, Figures and Tropes. *De arte metrica et de schematibus et tropis.* Edited by C. B. Kendall. CCSL 123A, pp. 59–171. Turnhout, Belgium: Brepols, 1975. Part II translated by G. H. Tanenhaus, "Bede's *De Schematibus et Tropis*—A Translation," *Quarterly Journal of Speech* 48 (1962):237–53. Reprinted in *Readings in Medieval Rhetoric.* Edited by Joseph M. Miller et al., pp. 76–80. Bloomington: Indiana University Press, 1973.

On Nature. *De natura rerum liber.* Edited by C. W. Jones. CCSL 123A, pp. 173–234. Turnhout, Belgium: Brepols, 1975.

Orthography. *De orthographia.* Edited by C. W. Jones. CCSL 123A, pp. 1–57. Turnhout, Belgium: Brepols, 1975.

Time and Chronicles. *De temporum ratione liber includens chronica maiora. De temporibus liber includens chronica minora.* Edited by C. W. Jones and T. Mommsen. CCSL 123B, 123C. Turnhout, Belgium: Brepols, 1977, 1980.

3. Biblical Commentaries and Topography

Acts. *Expositio Actuum Apostolorum, Retractatio in Actus Apostolorum.* Edited by M. L. W. Laistner. CCSL 121, pp. 1–163. Turnhout, Belgium: Brepols, 1983. Same as, but without the notes of, the edition printed for the Mediaeval Academy of America, no. 35. Cambridge, Mass: Mediaeval Academy of America, 1939.

Apocalypse. *Explanatio Apocalypsis.* PL 93.129–206.

Catholic Epistles. *In Epistolas VII Catholicas.* Edited by David Hurst. CCSL 121, pp. 179–342. Turnhout, Belgium: Brepols, 1983. Also *Bedae venerabilis explanatio Epistolae Iudae Apostoli.* Edited by Rand Haynie Johnson. Master's thesis, Brigham Young University, 1979. *The Commentary on the Seven Catholic Epistles.* Translated by David Hurst. Cistercian Studies no. 82. Kalamazoo, Mich.: Cistercian Publications, 1985.

Collectaneum on the Pauline Epistles. *Collectio Bedae presbyteri ex opusculis sancti Augustini in Epistulas Pauli Apostoli.* Still unprinted.

Eight Questions. *Aliquot quaestionum liber.* PL 93. 455–62. The remaining questions, 9–15 (cols. 462–78) are not by Bede.

Ezra and Nehemiah. *In Ezram et Neemiam.* Edited by D. Hurst. CCSL 119A, pp. 235–392. Turnhout, Belgium: Brepols, 1969.

Genesis. *Libri quatuor in principium Genesis usque ad nativitatem Isaac et eiectionem Ismahelis adnotationum.* Edited by C. W. Jones. CCSL 118A. Turnhout, Belgium: Brepols, 1967.

Habbakkuk. *In Habacuc.* Edited by J. E. Hudson. CCSL 119B, pp. 370–409. Turnhout, Belgium: Brepols, 1983.

Luke. *In Lucae evangelium expositio.* Edited by D. Hurst. CCSL 120, pp. 1–425. Turnhout, Belgium: Brepols, 1960.

Mark. *In Marci evangelium expositio.* Edited by D. Hurst. CCSL 120, pp. 427–648. Turnhout, Belgium: Brepols, 1960.

Proverbs. *In Proverbia.* Edited by D. Hurst. CCSL 119B, pp 21–163. Turnhout, Belgium: Brepols, 1983.

Sacred Places. *De locis sanctis.* Edited by F. Fraipont. In *Itineraria et alia geographica.* CCSL 175, pp. 245–80; 176, Index. Turnhout, Belgium: Brepols, 1965.

Samuel. *In primam partem Samuhelis libri IIII.* Edited by D. Hurst. CCSL 119, pp. 1–287. Turnhout, Belgium: Brepols, 1962.

Song of Songs. *In Cantica Canticorum.* Edited by D. Hurst. CCSL 119B, pp. 175–375. Turnhout, Belgium: Brepols, 1983.

Tabernacle. *De tabernaculo.* Edited by D. Hurst. CCSL 119A, pp. 1–139. Turnhout, Belgium: Brepols, 1979.

Temple. *De templo.* Edited by D. Hurst. CCSL 119A, pp. 141–234. Turnhout, Belgium: Brepols, 1979.

Thirty Questions. *In Regum librum XXX quaestiones.* Edited by D. Hurst. CCSL 119, pp. 289–322. Turnhout, Belgium: Brepols, 1972.

Tobit. *In Tobiam*. Edited by D. Hurst. CCSL 119B, pp. 1–19. Turnhout, Belgium: Brepols, 1983.

4. Homilies, Hagiography, Poems, Letters

Homilies. *Homeliarum evangelii libri II*. Edited by D. Hurst. CCSL 122, pp. 1–378. Turnhout, Belgium: Brepols, 1965.

Letter to Albinus. *Epistola ad Albinum*. In *Venerabilis Bedae opera historica*, edited by C. Plummer, I, p. [3]. Oxford: Oxford University Press, 1896.

Letter to Ecgbert. *Epistola ad Ecgbertum Episcopum*. In *Venerabilis Bedae opera historica*, edited by C. Plummer, I. pp. 405–23. In *EHD* I, no. 170, pp.799–810, translated by Dorothy Whitelock.

Letters to Plegwin, Helmwald, and Wicthed. *Epistolae ad Plegvinam, Helmvvaldum, et VVicthedum*. In *Opera didascalia*, part 3, edited by C. W. Jones. CCSL 123C, pp. 615–42. Turnhout, Belgium: Brepols, 1935.

Life of Cuthbert, in prose. *Vita sancti Cuthberti*. In *Two Lives of St. Cuthbert*, edited and translated by B. Colgrave. Cambridge: Cambridge University Press, 1940. Also in *Lives of the Saints*, edited and translated by J. F. Webb, pp. 69–129. Harmondsworth, England and Baltimore: Penguin, 1981.

Life of Cuthbert, in verse. *Bedas metrische vita sancti Cuthberti*, edited by Werner Jaager. Palaestra 198. Leipzig, Germany: Mayer and Müller, 1935).

Life of Felix. *A Critical Edition of Bede's Vita Felicis*. Edited by Thomas W. Mackay. Ph.D. dissertation, Stanford University, 1971; Ann Arbor, Mich.: University Microfilms, 1972.

Martyrology. *Édition practique des martyrologes de Bède, de l'anonyme lyonnais et de Florus*. Edited by Jacques DuBois and Geneviève Renaud. Paris: CNRS, 1976.

Poems. *Liber hymnorum, rhythmi, variae preces*. Edited by J. Fraipont. CCSL 122, pp. 405–70. Turnhout, Belgium: Brepols, 1965.

5. Histories

History of the Abbots of Wearmouth-Jarrow. *(HA) Vita beatorum abbatum Benedicti, Ceolfridi, Eostorwini, Sigfridi, atque Huaetherhti*. In *Venerabilis Baedae opera historica*, edited by C. Plummer, I, pp. 364–387. Oxford: Oxford University Press, 1896. Translation in Bede, *The Ecclesiastical History of the English People and Other Selections*, edited and translated by J. Campbell, pp. 371–96. New York: Washington Square Press, 1968. Also in *Bedae opera historica*, edited and translated by J. E. King, Loeb Classical Library, 2:392–445. London: William Heinemann, and New York: G. P. Putnam's Sons, 1930. (Not a good text or translation.)

The Ecclesiastical History of the English People. Bede's Ecclesiastical History of the English People. (*HE*) Edited with translation by Bertram Colgrave and R. A. B. Mynors. Oxford: Clarendon Press, 1969. Keyed to *Historica ecclesiastica gentis Anglorum*, in *Venerabilis Baedae opera historica.* Edited by Charles Plummer. 2 vols. Oxford: Oxford University Press, 1896. (Superlative introduction and notes.) Also *Bedae opera historica.* Edited by J. E. King. Loeb Classical Library. London: William Heinemann, and New York: G. P. Putnam's Sons, 1930. (Easily available but often inaccurate.) *A History of the English Church and People by Bede,* translated by L. Sherley-Price, revised by R. E. Latham. Harmondsworth, England, and Baltimore: Penguin, 1968. (A number of other translations exist.)

The Life of Ceolfrid. Historia Abbatum auctore Anonymo, in *Venerabilis Baedae opera historica,* edited by C. Plummer, I, pp. 388–404. Oxford: Oxford University Press, 1896. Translation in *The Life of Ceolfrid, Abbot of the Monastery at Wearmouth and Jarrow, by an Unknown Author of the Eighth Century,* translated by Douglas Samuel Boutflower. Sunderland, England: Hills and Company, 1912. Also in *Anglo-Saxon Saints and Heroes,* edited and translated by Clinton Albertson, S.J., pp. 247–71. New York: Fordham University Press, 1967. Also in *English Historical Documents, c.500–1042.* English Historical Documents, vol. I, edited by Dorothy Whitelock. 2d ed. no. 155, pp. 758–70. London: Eyre Methuen, and New York: Oxford University Press, 1979.

The Old English Version of Bede's Ecclesiastical History of the English People. Edited and translated by Thomas Miller. 2 parts in 3. Early English Text Society, original series, vols. 95, 96, 111. Oxford: Early English Text Society, 1890, 91, 98. Reprint. 1959.

SECONDARY SOURCES

1. Bibliographies

Anglo-Saxon England. Cambridge: Cambridge University Press, 1972– Annual bibliography of the previous year's work on Bede.

L'Année philologique. Paris: Société d'édition "Les belles lettres." This yearly critical analytic bibliography of Greco-Latin antiquity includes Bede and his age.

Bolton, Whitney F. "A Bede Bibliography: 1935–60." *Traditio* 18 (1962):437–45.

Bonser, Wilfred. *An Anglo-Saxon and Celtic Bibliography (450–1087).* Items 4154-4279, pp. 201–7, and Index. Berkeley: University of California Press, 1957.

Clavis patrum latinorum. Edited by E. Dekkers and A. Gaar. 2d edition. Items 1383-84, pp. 302–11. *Sacris Erudiri* no. 3. Steenbrugge, Belgium: St. Peter's Abbey, 1961.

Deutscher Gesamtkatalog herausgegeben von der preussischen Staatsbibliothek. Vol. 14, pp. 695–707. Berlin: Preussische Drückerei, 1939. For early editions of Bede.

Eckenrode, Thomas. "The Venerable Bede: A Bibliographical Essay, 1970–81." *American Benedictine Review* 36 (1985):172–91. Helpful despite inaccuracies and omissions.

Greenfield, Stanley B., and Fred C. Robinson. *A Bibliography of Publications on Old English Literature to the End of 1972.* Toronto: Toronto University Press, 1979.

Humphreys, K. W., and Alan S. C. Ross. "Further Manuscripts of Bede's 'Historia Ecclesiastica,' of the 'Epistola Cuthberti de Obitu Bedae,' and Further Anglo-Saxon Texts of 'Cædmon's Hymn' and 'Bede's Death Song.' " *Notes & Queries,* n. s. 22 (1975):50–55.

International Medieval Bibliography. Edited by Richard J. Walsh. Leeds: University of Leeds, 1967–. Lists articles and notes on medieval topics from over a thousand sources; each year contains ten to twelve entries on Bede.

Jones, Charles W. *Bedae Pseudepigrapha: Scientific Writings Falsely Attributed to Bede.* Ithaca, N.Y.: Cornell University Press, 1939.

Laistner, M. L. W., and H. H. King. *A Hand-List of Bede Manuscripts.* Ithaca, N.Y.: Cornell University Press, 1943.

MLA International Bibliography of Books and Articles on the Modern Languages and Literatures. Vol. 1. New York: Modern Language Association of America. Bede is included under English Literature/400–1099, and elsewhere as a topic (consult subject index).

The New Cambridge Bibliography of English Literature. Edited by George Watson. Vol. 1. Cambridge: Cambridge University Press, 1974.

Old English Newsletter. Binghamton, New York: 1967– .

Potthast, August, et al. *Repertorium fontium historiae medii aevi.* Rev. ed. Vol. 2, pp. 429–73. Rome: Istituto storico italiano, 1962. Includes earlier scholarship.

Rosenthal, Joel T. *Anglo-Saxon History: An Annotated Bibliography, 450–1066.* New York: AMS Press, 1985. Historiographical, not literary. Helpful annotations.

Stegmüller, Friedrich. *Repertorium biblicum medii aevi.* Vol. 2, 174–193; vol. 8 (supplement), 339–47. Madrid: Instituto Francesco Suárez,

1950, 1956. Lists the Bedan and pseudo-Bedan commentaries on Scripture, with their incipits.

See also the excellent but now dated (1970) select bibliography in Peter Hunter Blair's *World of Bede,* listed below.

2. Books

Bonner, Gerald, ed. *Famulus Christi: Essays in Commemoration of the Thirteenth Centenary of the Birth of the Venerable Bede.* London: SPCK, 1976. This worthy sequel to the Thompson volume contains twenty-two essays, all highly instructive.

Browne, George F. *The Venerable Bede: His Life and Writings.* London: SPCK, 1919. Anecdotal, misleading.

Campbell, James, ed. *The Anglo-Saxons.* Ithaca, N.Y.: Cornell University Press, 1982. A beautiful volume with splendid essays and illustrations.

Carroll, Sr. M. Thomas Aquinas. *The Venerable Bede: His Spiritual Teachings.* Catholic University of America Studies in Medieval History, n.s., 9. Washington, D. C.: Catholic University of America Press, 1946. One of the few works to analyze Bede's exegesis, but only with an emphasis on the ascetical aspects. Good on Bede's doctrine and devotion.

De Lubac, Henri. *Exégèse médiévale: les quatre sens de l'Écriture.* 2 vols. in 4. Paris: Aubier, 1959–64. The most complete survey of allegorical interpretation of the Bible, but with no special section on Bede's exegesis.

Duckett, Eleanor Shipley. *Anglo-Saxon Saints and Scholars.* New York: Macmillan, 1947. Chapter 3 is on Bede. Popular narrative.

Farmer, Hugh. "The Studies of Anglo-Saxon Monks (A.D. 600–800)." In *Los monjes y los estudios: IV semana de estudios monasticos,* Poblet, 1961. Poblet, Spain: Abadia de Poblet, 1963.

Farrell, Robert T., ed. *Bede and Anglo-Saxon England: Papers in Honour of the 1300th Anniversary of the Birth of Bede, Given at Cornell University in 1973 and 1974.* British Archaeological Reports, 46. Oxford: British Archaeological Reports, 1978. Essays by D. M. Wilson on art and architecure of Bedan Northumbria, Winthrop Wetherbee on Bede's style, and Patrick Wormald on Bede and *Beowulf.*

Greenfield, Stanley B., and Daniel G. Calder. *A New Critical History of Old English Literature.* New York: New York University Press, 1986. (Supersedes Greenfield's *A Critical History of Old English Literature* [New York: New York University Press, 1965], also used in this study.) This authoritative handbook contains a survey chapter of the Anglo-Latin background, including Bede and his works, by Michael

Lapidge, as well as discussions of the Old English *HE*, *Cædmon's Hymn*, and Bede's Death Song.

Hanning, Robert W. *The Vision of History in Early Britain: From Gildas to Geoffrey of Monmouth.* New York: Columbia University Press, 1966.

Harrison, Kenneth. *The Framework of Anglo-Saxon History.* Cambridge: Cambridge University Press, 1976. Most accurate analysis of Anglo-Saxon dates and dating.

Hunter Blair, Peter. *Anglo-Saxon Northumbria.* Edited by Michael Lapidge and Pauline Hunter Blair. London: Variorum Reprints, 1984. Twelve published papers (1939–76) relevant to Bede, conveniently collected.

————. *Northumbria in the Days of Bede.* New York: St. Martin's Press, 1976. A lively, popular presentation.

————. *The World of Bede.* London: Secker & Warburg, 1970. One of the best books on Bede and his milieu.

The Jarrow Lectures. Jarrow, England: Rector of Jarrow, 1958– . Each year an eminent Bedan scholar delivers the Jarrow lecture on some aspect of Bede and his England; it is then published in this excellent series. Many of the lectures are cited in the chapter notes.

King, Margot H., and Wesley M. Stevens, eds. *Saints, Scholars, and Heroes: Studies in Medieval Culture in Honour of Charles W. Jones.* Vol. 1, The Anglo-Saxon Heritage. Collegeville, Minn.: St. John's Abbey and University, 1979. Several good articles relevant to Bede.

Laistner, M. L. W. *The Intellectual Heritage of the Early Middle Ages.* Edited by Chester G. Starr. Ithaca, N.Y.: Cornell University Press, 1957. Includes four previously published, important essays on Bede.

————. *Thought and Letters in Western Europe.* A.D. *500 to 900.* Ithaca, N.Y.: Cornell University Press, 1966. Still the best general introduction to early medieval culture.

Mayr-Harting, Henry. *The Coming of Christianity to England.* New York: Schocken Books, 1972. A fresh and stimulating history.

Meyvaert, Paul. *Benedict, Gregory, Bede and Others.* London: Variorum Reprints, 1977. Items 8–12 are previously published pieces on Bede by this eminent scholar.

Musca, Giosuè. *Il venerabile Beda, storico dell'alto medioevo.* Bari, Italy: Dedalo Libri, 1973. Sensitive to Bede as exegete.

Riché, Pierre. *Education and Culture in the Barbarian West from the Sixth through the Eighth Century.* Translated by John J. Contreni. Columbia: University of South Carolina Press, 1976.

Southern, R. W. *Medieval Humanism and Other Studies.* Oxford: Basil Blackwell, 1970. Chapter 1 (pp. 1–8) is a brief, elegant essay on Bede.

Stenton, Frank M. *Anglo-Saxon England.* 3d ed. Oxford: Clarendon Press, 1971. Remains the single most authoritative history of the period.

Thompson, A. Hamilton, ed. *Bede: His Life, Times, and Writings: Essays in Commemoration of the Twelfth Centenary of His Death.* Oxford: Clarendon Press, 1935. Reprint. 1969. Great essays, especially those by Levison, Colgrave, and Laistner, but now dated in nearly every respect.

Wallace—Hadrill, J. M. *Early Germanic Kingship in England and on the Continent.* The Ford Lectures at the University of Oxford, 1970. Oxford: Clarendon Press, 1971. Chapter 4, "Bede," shows Bede's dependence on the Bible, Eusebius, Gregory, Isidore, and Gildas for his notions of Anglo-Saxon kingship.

Werner, Karl. *Beda der Ehrwürdige und seine Zeit.* 2d ed. Vienna: Wilhelm Braumüller, 1881. The first really scholarly investigation of Bede; largely superseded.

Whitelock, Dorothy. *English Historical Documents, 500–1042.* English Historical Documents, Vol. I. 2d ed. London: Eyre Methuen; New York: Oxford University Press, 1979. With excellent introduction and commentaries, a peerless collection of sources, including the *Life of Ceolfrith,* much of *HE,* and letters.

——— . *From Bede to Alfred.* London: Variorum Reprints, 1980. Previously published essays; chap. 5 on Bede, chaps. 8 and 9 on the Old English version of *HE.*

Wormald, Patrick, with Donald Bullough, and Roger Collins, eds. *Ideal and Reality in Frankish and Anglo-Saxon Society: Studies Presented to J. M. Wallace-Hadrill.* Oxford: Basil Blackwell, 1983. This festschrift contains four fine articles (chaps. 4–7) on Bede by J. McClure, A. Thacker, C. Stancliffe, and P. Wormald.

3. Articles

Bischoff, Bernhard. "Turning-Points in the History of Latin Exegesis in the Early Irish Church: A.D. 650–800." In *Biblical Studies: The Medieval Irish Contribution.* Proceedings of the Irish Biblical Association, no. 1. Dublin: Dominican Publications, 1976. Important for understanding Bede's theological orientation.

Brown, T. Julian. "An Historical Introduction to the Use of Classical Latin Authors in the British Isles from the Fifth to the Eleventh Centuries." In *La cultura antica nell'occidente latino dal VII all'XI seccolo,* 1:238–99. Settimane di studio del centro italiano de studi sull'alto medioevo, no. 22. Spoleto, Italy: Presso la sede del centro, 1975.

Campbell, James. "Bede." In *Latin Historians,* edited by T. A. Dorey. London: Routledge & Kegan Paul, 1966. Integrates Bede's roles as teacher and exegete with that of historian.

Capelle, P. "Le rôle théologique de Bède le Vénérable." *Studia Anselmiana*

6 (1936):1–40. One of the earliest efforts to assess Bede as a theologian.

Colgrave, Bertram. "The Earliest Saints' Lives Written in England." *Proceedings of the British Academy* 44 (1958):35–60.

Davidse, Jan. "The Sense of History in the Works of the Venerable Bede." *Studi Medievali* 23 (1982):664–70. One of the most illuminating investigations into Bede's exegetical historical synthesis.

Dionisotti, Anna Carlotta. "On Bede, Grammars, and Greek." *Revue Benedictine* 92 (1982):11–41. Brilliantly establishes the nature of Bede's *On Orthography*.

Jones, Charles W. "Some Introductory Remarks on Bede's Commentary on Genesis." *Sacris Erudiri* 19 (1969–70):115–98. Good treatment of Bede's allegorical exegesis.

Lapidge, Michael. "Some Remnants of Bede's Lost *Liber Epigrammatum*." *English Historical Review* 90 (1975):798–820. Argues that the codex formerly owned by Bishop Milred of Worcester contains some genuine samples of Bede's epigrams.

Leonardi, Claudio. "Il venerabile Beda e la cultura del secolo VIII." In *I problemi dell'occidente nel secolo VIII*, pp. 603–58. Settimane di studio del centro italiano di studi sull'alto medioevo, no. 20. Spoleto, Italy: Presso la sede del centro, 1973. Discusses Bede's "mystic monastic" outlook.

McClure, Judith. "Bede and the Life of Ceolfrid" *Peritia* 3 (1984):71–84. Argues for Bede's authorship.

—————. "Bede's *Notes on Genesis* and the Training of the Anglo-Saxon Clergy." In *The Bible in the Medieval World: Essays in Memory of Beryl Smalley*, edited by Katherine Walsh and Diana Wood, pp. 17–30. Oxford: Basil Blackwell, 1985.

Martin, Lawrence T. "Bede as a Linguistic Scholar." *American Benedictine Review* 35 (1984):204–17.

Olsen, Glenn W. "From Bede to the Anglo-Saxon Presence in the Carolingian Empire." In *Angli e Sassoni al di qua e al di là del mare nell'alto medioevo*. Settimane di studio del centro italiano di studi sull'alto medioevo, no. 32, forthcoming. Spoleto, Italy: Presso la sede del centro, 1986. Perceptive analysis of Bede's individuality.

Palmer, Robert B. "Bede as a Textbook Writer: A Study of His *De Arte Metrica*." *Speculum* 34 (1959):573–84. The first modern critic to appreciate and analyze with some detail Bede's abilities as an educational writer.

Ray, Roger. "Augustine's *De Consensu Evangelistarum* and the Historical Education of the Venerable Bede." In *Studia Patristica* 16, part 2. Texte und Untersuchungen zur Geschichte der altchristlichen Literatur, vol. 129 (1985), 557–63.

————. "Bede's *Vera Lex Historiae.*" *Speculum* 55 (1980):1–21. Points out Bede's own meaning for Jerome's phrase, to allow common report as historical evidence.

————. "What Do We Know about Bede's Commentaries?" *Recherches de théologie ancienne et médiévale* 49 (1982):5–20.

Rosenthal, Joel T. "Bede's Use of Miracles in His 'Ecclesiastical History,' " *Traditio* 31 (1975):328–35. Points out that the miracle stories occur mostly in books IV and V, and explains why.

Schindel, Ulrich. "Die Quellen von Bedas Figurenlehre." *Classica et Mediaevalia* 29 (1968):170–86. A careful catalogue of the sources used by Bede in his *On Figures*.

Stephens, J. N. "Bede's Ecclesiastical History." *History* 62 (1977):1–14. A challenging, intelligent, if not totally convincing article.

Strubel, Armand. " 'Allegoria in factis' et 'Allegoria in verbis.' " *Poétique* 23 (1975):342–57. A modern critical analysis of Bede's allegorical categories.

Willmes, Ansgar. "Bedas Bibelauslegung." *Archiv für Kulturgeschichte* 44 (1963):281–314. Discusses not only Bede's exegetical methods but his influence in the later Middle Ages.

Index

AUTHOR INDEX